Findhorn
Reflections:

A very personal take on life
inside the famous spiritual
community and ecovillage

Graham Meltzer

Meltzer's honest and inspiring insights on life in a spiritual community makes a very good read!   Penny Johnston

Graham Meltzer is a fantastic writer and his ideas are wonderful!   Dorota Owen

I applaud the author's authentic sharing on such an open and personal level.   Peter Wolff

Controversial, moving and enlightening all at the same time! Wonderful!   Catherine Brislee

ISBN-13: 978-1512006513
ISBN-10: 1512006513

DEDICATION

To my community

CONTENTS

INTRODUCTION

Welcome to my world – life inside the famous spiritual community and ecovillage in Findhorn, North Scotland. I've been living here for almost ten years now, having come from Australia where I lived for 30 years after first growing up in New Zealand. I hope that the contents of this book make it clear why I chose and continue to live in such a remote location with a relatively harsh climate when I could be living closer to much loved family in the sub-tropics. I love my life here, else I would surely be back in Australia or NZ.

I am fully ensconced in the Findhorn Foundation and community, enamoured of the lifestyle and committed to remain for the foreseeable future. Yet in some ways I'm somewhat of an alien; I didn't take readily to some of the more esoteric aspects of the culture. I came to Findhorn seeking a socially satisfying, ecologically benign community life, not to deepen a spiritual journey or to communicate with nature spirits. So my personal take on the life here is both a love letter and a critique. And it's also a story of my own personal growth and transformation as wrought by the 'magic of Findhorn.'

The 'Findhorn Foundation and Community' (as we prefer to be known) began in November, 1962 when the three founders, Eileen Caddy, Peter Caddy and Dorothy Maclean first settled in Findhorn with the Caddy's three children, Christopher, Jonathan and David. It could perhaps be said that a mini-community began ten years earlier when the three came together to deepen their shared spiritual journey, which later was to become the foundation stone of the community. In Peter's words, 'during the previous ten years every action of our lives had been directed by guidance from the voice of God within.' God spoke to them via messages that Eileen channelled in meditation.

And so it was, after life harshly dumped them in the Findhorn Bay Holiday Park, that Eileen's guidance continued to shape every aspect and determine every detail of their lives. Because they were flat broke, surviving only on Peter's unemployment benefit of £8 per week, they started a garden in which to grow food. Soon after, Dorothy too began to receive messages, which she attributed to the plant kingdom. She first contacted what she referred to as the *deva* or spirit of the garden pea, then went on to communicate with devas of many more plant species as well as elementals and unseen beings of different kinds. Most of these messages were practical – where, when and what to plant, how to make compost, etc. Peter would enact the guidance, developing the garden, seeking to 'co-create with the intelligence of nature,' as they perceived it. Soon enough they began to enjoy remarkable success, growing an abundance of oversized, healthy organic produce in very unlikely conditions – barren soil in a hostile environment. With the aid of modest publicity that Peter disseminated, visitors started arriving to see and hear what this was all about. Some of them stayed on. And, as they say, the rest is history. Even though the founders never intended or even imagined founding a new community, a community formed around them, and it grew, and it grew.

Today, something like 700 members live in and around 'The Park,' as it's called. The community is diverse in its demographic, complex in its organisation and rich in its social and cultural milieu. I hope that this book can offer a glimpse of the present day 'magic of Findhorn' and also highlight some of the challenges we face as a 50 year old intentional community, born of the '60s as a harbinger of the New Age.

This book comprises somewhat unrelated chapters, each a vignette of an aspect of community life. Most of them began life as a post on my blog, Findhornblog.wordpress.com. They fall into three broad themes, which form the three parts of the book. 'Part One: Inner Work' is about our shared spirituality and my personal spiritual deepening, in particular. We often talk in Findhorn of the inner work we do (on our ego, principally) in order to lead a more authentic life and one that best contributes to the 'highest and the best' for all; this section describes my own such journey via some of our beliefs and practices. 'Part Two: Outer Work' is about the 'glue' of community life – our relationships. Communal living is intense and challenging at the best of times. Without successful relationship building and dispute resolution techniques, a community will soon fail and fall apart. This section focuses on some aspects of our social and cultural milieu which perhaps underpin our success and others which I believe can still be improved upon. 'Part Three: World Work' is about our contribution to the world beyond. As well as being a spiritual community and an ecovillage, we are also an educational centre. We run programmes continuously, hosting some 12,000 residential guests annually, many of whom undergo profound life-changing experiences. We are, as we like to say, 'changing the world one heart at a time.'

The book completes with two chapters that are a homage to Scotland, my adopted homeland. So the trajectory of the book moves from the personal, through the interpersonal to the world beyond. That each of these three realms has been couched in terms of 'work,' should not be too surprising. To us, work has little of the mundane about it. On the contrary, we see all work as 'love in action' – an opportunity for service to the highest and the best. I hope that in some small way, this book inspires readers to aim for nothing less in their own lives.

PART ONE

INNER WORK

1

A SPIRITUAL LIFE?

I'm amused that the first chapter should focus on my spirituality because I arrived in Findhorn ten years ago with a strongly material and sceptical worldview. I believed I was without a spiritual bone in my body; a stance I had held since childhood. By the age of 12, I'd decided there was no such thing as a (Judeo-Christian) God – that the whole notion was simply a construct. I did so for the same reasons given recently by Stephen Fry; the notion of an omniscient, omnipotent, beneficent God makes no sense to me given the levels of chaos, pain and strife in the world. I have likewise never believed in an afterlife. I studied science at school and university and in time became a social scientist. I still value the scientific method, take nothing at face value and seek evidence for any phenomenon that stretches my credulity (such as angels, devas and nature spirits, for those of you who already know about Findhornian culture).

So perhaps not surprisingly, I struggled as a teenager to make sense of life, convinced that there was no heaven, no God-given guidance by which one lives, indeed no ostensible meaning to life! So I researched, seeking meaning in moral philosophy, political theory and existentialist literature. And I reasoned. I decided that if the gift of life on this Earth is all there is, then I damned well better make the most of it, else waste a unique and precious opportunity. I gradually developed a humanist worldview, recognising that we humans are born with enormous potential for growth, development and magnificent achievement. And yet sadly, most of us never realize more than what? 10%? 5%? 1% of that potential? I started to see unfulfilled human potential as that which provides meaning to life.

Ultimately, I came up with a home-spun ethos of my own by which I believed I could live and make sense of my life. I reasoned that *creativity* is a key potential that remains unfulfilled in most people. We are innately a creative species, evidenced by our extraordinary cultural development. Surely, creativity is one of our primary drives as a species. And yet, as individuals most of us rarely tap our creative potential. So I resolved, there and then, to strive as best I could to develop my creativity. But, I reasoned, this can be quite an individualistic, self-centred pursuit. Having read the kind of left wing political literature prevalent in the sixties, I had developed a strong socialist/egalitarian streak (one for all and all for one). The notion of a self-absorbed drive to realize one's unique creative potential worried me.

The principle of *service* seemed to offer a balance. If developing one's creativity was about meeting the needs of the individual then service offered the opportunity to give something back. So it seemed equally important to realize one's potential in service – to family, community, society and the planet. Happy with that, I still felt there was something missing – something that tied these two impulses together, integrating them somehow. *Love* provided the answer. I reasoned that whatever one does, should be done with love. And that the third imperative by which I would live my life would be to deepen into love in all its various manifestations. I would pursue greater creativity *with love*; and I would seek to serve *with love*. And I would love *with love*.

So there you have it – my home-spun, tripartite, *raison d'être*. I saw these three impulses: *creativity*, *service* and *love*, as a kind of holy trinity. Developing my potential in these three arenas would be my purpose, my code of conduct and my 'religion.' And so it's been all my life. Whenever I have a decision to make, large or small, I assess it against these three criteria and decided accordingly. I ask, 'What choice will enable me to best grow creativity, service and/or love?' It's as easy and as difficult as that.

The relevance of all this to Findhorn, I think, lies in the congruence that I feel here in this community. At Findhorn, we similarly value creativity, service and love; indeed, these are three central tenets to our community's spirituality. It could be said that our key mantra, 'work is love in action' synthesises these three aspects of our culture. We see all work as an act of *service*. We seek to bring *love* to everything we do by being fully present and totally engaged. And action, certainly as it was modelled by Peter Caddy, is *creativity* made manifest.

Herein lays the source of my contentment at Findhorn. Living in this community enables greater alignment between my values and my lifestyle. This, for me, is crucial to my personal wellbeing. Furthermore, living here has enriched my daily life. It has provided practices that enable me to further cultivate my purpose. As the practices have become second nature, so my contentment has deepened. What's more, living in this community for ten years has softened my worldview, a lot! Much of that change has occurred in the last few years. It took its time, but eventually Findhorn worked its magic on my somewhat limited, sceptical worldview. And I'm extremely grateful for that.

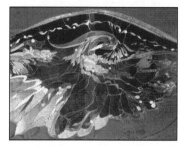 

2

MY HOME

Eight years ago, I had the privilege of designing and building the home I have lived in ever since. The interior spaces in particular were designed to deliver qualities appropriate for coworkers of a spiritual community, whom often-times seek peace and tranquillity in their dwellings, away from the intensity of community life. The house is designed as a space of retreat; a place of psychological and spiritual nurture. For most of us who work in the Findhorn Foundation, community life is very busy, often intense. Every day we interact closely with guests, many of whom we meet as strangers. This can be very challenging, especially for an introvert like me. And of course it's also very rewarding. But it requires (for me anyway) that I have a home to return to in the evening where I can recharge my batteries.

The building of my house, I think it can be said, was a perfect application of the tripartite ethos I wrote of in the previous chapter; it was an exercise in fulfilling my potential for creativity, service and love. To design and build a house is, for me, the ultimate act of creativity. It's sculpting on a grand scale. And that the final outcome, the artefact, is then inhabited, makes it all the more rewarding. It's not just an *objet d'art* but has function, purpose and the potential to significantly improve people's lives. I did the work (if you can call it that) as an act of service, working for the Findhorn Foundation in my job in the Assets Area which oversees design and building in the Foundation. I worked extremely hard, mostly single handed, for eight months through the middle of winter. And yet throughout the build, I could permit myself no expectation of being able to live in the house when completed. In the Foundation, we make decisions about who will move into a house or occupy a room in a shared house at the time it becomes available. At that point, those coworkers who are interested meet for an *attunement* during which the decision is made, in good part, on the basis of guidance received during meditation. (See Chapter Six, *Going Within* for more detail.) Sometimes, the outcome of an attunement can be counter intuitive or may even seem unjust. Attunements are not necessarily predicated on natural justice. But, as it turns out, I prevailed in the attunement and have been happily living in the house ever since.

Finally, I can truly say that I did the work as an act of love. I very much love to design and equally to build. Both activities, I find deeply nourishing and fulfilling and when they're combined, the joy and satisfaction I derive is all the more profound. When I'm working, I become focussed to the point of obsession on every little detail. The famous German architect, Mies van der Rohe coined the phrase, 'God is in the detail' for good reason. In the activity of designing and building not just the macro, but particularly the detail, I come close to a state of divine bliss (if I'm allowed to say that as an atheist).

The building is located in an area of high ecological value and sensitivity where numerous full-grow specimen trees form a nature corridor linking two areas of wildlife habitat. Because the building has a small footprint and 'touches the ground lightly' (resting as it does on just a few pad footings) it can be set amongst the trees with minimal impact. It's what we call, an 'ecomobile' i.e. a residential building, built to the regulations governing caravans and mobile homes. So technically it's a caravan, but one that's built in situ with a high ecological specification. There are several such buildings in the area.

The entrance is approached across a bridge and under a pergola that carries climbing roses. A conservatory cum entry porch constructed of reclaimed doors and windows clad in translucent polycarbonate provides a space to gently arrive and deposit coats and shoes. It's lit at night with colour-changing LEDs that offer a light show to passers-by in the street. The progression from street to interior across a bridge (a metaphor for transitioning from one world to another) is designed as a series of experiences that encourage a subtle energy and mood shift from that of the busy outside world to a more relaxed and tranquil state of being.

The building comprises: a single main living space, a separate bedroom and a link between them incorporating a bathroom and storage. The main space has an octagonal floor plan. Its form and minimalist detailing induce a feeling of ease, comfort and nurture. The 135 degree corners are more subtle and easier on the eye than conventional 90 degree ones. Within the space, separate kitchen, dining and living areas pinwheel about a centrally located wood stove, symbolic of a primeval hearth or firepit. Each area borrows space and amenity from the others, enabling a smaller combined footprint. Large windows and a central skylight deliver high levels of natural light.

The linking corridor too, is flooded with daylight entering through its translucent roof and ceiling. With full-length storage along one side, it doubles as a dressing room. A small but well-appointed bathroom incorporates toilet, basin and shower. Because clothes are stored elsewhere, the bedroom is minimally furnished (with just a bed). Its pure cubic form, high ceiling and minimalist décor induce, to my mind, the qualities of a 'sacred' space. A full-width South-facing clerestory lets in sun and light, and invites views of the stars and full moon. A narrow full-height window to the West offers views of nearby trees. An East-facing deck opens off the bedroom, incorporating a hammock and an *ofuro* for two (Japanese style hot tub) made from a whisky barrel.

The building cost approximately £40,000 to construct. At £800 per m^2, that's about half the construction cost of new-built, architect designed and detailed homes in the region. The biggest cost saving was achieved through self-building. The labour component of the overall cost was approximately 20% – considerably less than normal. I built the house alone but help from the community was always at hand when I needed it. Since I was both designer and builder, this reduced the amount of documentation necessary and eliminated any need for conventional architectural supervision. Further savings were made through online shopping for materials, fixtures and fittings. This resulted in many fewer trips to local service centres in order to buy construction materials, saving time, money and carbon emissions.

The building is, in truth, poorly oriented for passive solar gain. Site constraints dictated that it be elongated in a North-South direction, counter to passive solar design principles. However, the South facing conservatory and large openings on South-facing walls provide considerable passive solar gain. Heating is provided by a wood stove burning firewood from our own forest. The boiler is electric. The cook top is a low-energy induction hob. There is no television, washing machine, clothes dryer, dishwasher or microwave. Because the building creates no carbon emissions in its day to day running (the electricity is generated by our own windmills), it can be considered a 'zero-carbon' building. And it probably has the lowest running costs of any building in the ecovillage.

To summarise, the house is a vehicle for sustainable living. Designed for a single person or a couple, it offers high levels of comfort and amenity whilst enabling the occupants to minimise their environmental footprint. The building is about half the size (per person) of the average UK dwelling. Small dwellings require fewer materials to construct, less energy to heat, and can hold less material 'stuff.' Beyond material considerations, however, it offers a supportive setting for 'voluntary simplicity' – a less consumerist, more conscious and environmentally benign lifestyle characterised by ease and beauty. A setting for a contemplative life; a place where the soul may find peace.

3

ON DIET

In an excellent article titled, 'Changing Stories: Using narrative to shift societal values,' Jonathan Dawson reminds us that the path to a transformation of consciousness and values is one that can only be discovered in the walking, in the *doing*. Concrete change generally lays in the *practice* – not in the ideas, nor the theorising or the esoterica. In Chapter 1, I outlined my ethos for living, a theory of sorts. In the second chapter, I described my home, the context for my domestic life. In this one, I begin to discuss my practices, which as Dawson says, is what really counts when it comes to personal change. It's where the rubber meets the road, as they say. And in my case, I have experienced profound transformation since coming to Findhorn, in several different facets of my life, not least that of diet.

Since the mid 1980s, I've begun a typical working day at three or four in the morning. I've always enjoyed working in the stillness of the early morning, when for me. the mind is fresh and at it's most creative, often hatching ideas that have incubated overnight. I'll work for two or three hours then take breakfast. And this is where my daily spiritual practice begins, with breakfast. How so? Well for me, diet is integral to spirituality. In the last few years, as my awareness has deepened, I've gradually been refining my diet. As mentioned in Chapter 1, alignment or congruence is crucial to my wellbeing, as is diet of course from the health and fitness perspective. But the motivation to improve my diet has mostly come in the pursuit of congruence, not improved health.

It began about five years ago when I gave up alcohol. I'd been drinking since I was 12 or 13 and had always enjoyed whisky in particular (an inheritance from my dad). Indeed, I 'had a habit'. So coming to live in Scotland was always going to be dangerous. And so it proved; I gained a whole new appreciation of the local Speyside produce. The river Spey is just down the road from Findhorn; it's waters inspire the most prolific whisky production in the land. At some point however, probably after admitting to myself that I was a borderline alcoholic, I decided to quit. And so I did, there and then, overnight. I simply decided that I would no longer have my resistant mind overruled by my bodily cravings for the stuff.

I was delighted to find that giving up was easy – I had no physical withdrawal symptoms whatsoever and anyway seemed to possess a surfeit of will power. So I reasoned that I was probably not physiologically addicted after all; I simply had a bad habit. The main benefit was also a surprise; I felt incredibly liberated. I learned of the tremendous freedom in being free from desire and craving. The change brought me into a whole new relationship with my body. I gained an appreciation of the value of congruence or alignment between mind and body i.e. of not having physical desires dictate to a mind that knows better.

A year or two later, I undertook a 10 day juice fast. The motivation was weight loss. I was feeling the dietary consequences of a long and harsh winter – an overload of carbs and a scarcity of fresh greens. In our climate, given our preference at Findhorn for eating locally and seasonally, we enjoy an abundance of fabulous vegetables and salads from our gardens in summer, but suffer from the opposite in winter. (And many of us avoid, minimise or boycott shopping in Tesco for produce from all parts of the world.) Anyway, the fast went well; I enjoyed the clean out. It didn't result in much weight loss, but it did deliver further realisations. It deepened my appreciation of what my body really needed and firmed my resolve to act in response.

I gave up caffeine immediately, having had a serious coffee habit for some 30 years – a habit that began when I studied architecture and needed to get through 'all nighters.' Later, coffee fuelled my mainstream lifestyle. Even after coming to Findhorn and adopting a more measured way of life, I continued to need several strong espressos to kick start the day. I was hooked! And yet once again, I was able to quit without difficulty, both coffee and black tea. Since then, I've kept a coffee pot on the hob but use it only for guests.

By then, the ball was rolling; I was on a health kick. I wondered what could be the next level of dietary divestment. At the time, I was reading of the evils of refined sugar. This seemed like the next logical step – to give up cakes, biscuits and puddings. And it seemed like it would be the toughest call yet. I love desserts in particular, and our Findhorn kitchen crew make them to die for. Furthermore, I was soon to go to Australia to spend time with my mum. I guess I must associate puddings with mothers' love at some deep psychological level. So I decided to postpone giving up sugar until after my six month sabbatical in Oz. But the universe provided an unexpected twist. When I arrived there, I found that mum had herself, only recently given up sugar. She was no longer baking cakes and making puddings. So clearly, it was 'meant to be.' I gratefully grabbed the opportunity and did likewise. Once again, giving up was easy. There were no subsequent unmet cravings. It seemed as though my mind had switched off that particular impulse. So whilst I strongly believe that I have an addictive personality, it seems I am able to deal readily with abstinence. I think the cravings must reside in my mind rather than my body – be psychological rather than physiological.

Whilst I was in Australia, I took advantage of the gym, sauna and pool in my mother's apartment building. I worked out daily and dropped almost 10 kg, returning to Scotland feeling fitter and healthier than I had for 20 or 30 years. That was a year and a half ago. More recently, with the influence of a certain woman in my life, I have released several more long-held dietary preferences and moved quite rapidly toward becoming vegan. I have been a poorly committed vegetarian for 40 years, avoiding red meat but with a strong attachment to eating fish, eggs and cheese – even chicken occasionally. These days, I eat little of the above. And I'm really benefiting, health wise. Sinus congestion I've endured for decades has almost completely disappeared, along with the mild asthma that it induced. My digestion has improved and I'm sleeping more soundly, despite having been a chronic insomniac since the 1980s.

In terms of the congruence I spoke of, I feel there is now little else to achieve in respect of diet. There is nothing more to give up. The process I've described, which may not sound like a spiritual path to some, has been central to my soul's journey. My body and my mind have finally made peace; no longer are there substances that the former desires but the latter resists. This brings a great deal of inner stillness and contentment which, for me, creates a platform for deepening into spiritual practice.

4

CARDS

The first three chapters have featured my inner and domestic life; I haven't yet ventured beyond my front door. There's been little reference to the community or culture of Findhorn, which ostensibly is what this book is about. But as a postscript to the preceding chapters, I'd like to emphasise that much of what I have discussed so far has a context – the culture, dynamics and life of the Findhorn community. There is little (perhaps nothing) of which I write that can be taken in isolation. In community, everything is interconnected. This is true more generally I believe, but in community the interconnectedness is patently evident.

So for example, the house in which I live would not have been built but for a specific set of conditions including a need for staff housing at the time and an enormous amount of community support, encouragement and resources. And similarly, my dietary journey has only been possible with the support of partners, family, friends, and colleagues. My organic, sugar-free and vegan food preferences are supported both by our community shop which stocks the alternative foodstuffs I need to cook at home, and the kitchen staff who dream up and produce the fabulous meals in our Community Centre (CC). I typically eat there twice a day (lunch and dinner) and always there are 'alternatives' provided for people on specialist diets or with particular preferences.

This, to my mind, is the inherent power of community – the way in which the collective can support the individual to become who they wish to be. And of course, it's reciprocal – the members serve the collective, seeking to achieve the highest and the best outcomes for the community as a whole. At least, that's the ideal. In practice, of course, it's not so easy; we all have an ego that will make its own demands.

This chapter is about one of my spiritual practices that would not exist but for Findhorn; it was born and bred in the community. On my living room table is a box labelled Intuitive Solutions; it contains three types of cards: Insight, Setback and Angel cards. The tag line on the box reads, 'A Tool for Inspired Action.' Angel cards are well known around the world and closely associated with Findhorn. The other two types are perhaps less well known. The instruction book contains the following paragraph:

> [This set of cards offers] a quick way to gain immediate understanding and direction. It enhances your creativity by helping you to dive deeply into a concern, think through difficulties, and make decisions in harmony with your values and integrity. You can use Intuitive Solutions to break through inertia and express your wisdom and clarity.

The cards were originally devised as an integral part of a board game called the Game of Life, later renamed the Transformation Game. The game was invented in the late 1970s by Findhorn members Joy Drake and Kathy Tyler as a means of simulating the Findhorn experience elsewhere. Without having to come here, people around the world could learn the lessons and gain the insights that an immersive Findhorn experience provides. Nowadays, the cards are available for use separately from the game. They can be used in many different ways but I use them as follows.

Every morning after breakfast, often as I'm running late to

get to Taizé singing (see the following chapter), I draw four cards in strict sequence: an Insight card, followed by a Setback, then another Insight and finally an Angel card. Before doing so, I take a moment to 'tune in' i.e. align with a purpose or intention for the day or simply ask a question I might have about something that's up for me. The message written on the first Insight card will prompt reflections that support the purpose or intention or perhaps answer the question. The Setback card will suggest an obstacle, personal limitation or impediment that might set me back in the process. And the second Insight card will suggest ways in which I might deal with the setback. Finally, the Angel card will suggest a quality that I might bring to the situation to assist in implementing the insights.

It is a very intuitive process which I notice I'm struggling to explain clearly. What the process is not, is scientific. It's mysterious. So I can imagine that you, the reader who has heard about my sceptical world view, are wondering at this point about my sanity. Drawing cards like this is something I would have run a mile from for most of my life. I think I got burned during my hippie years. I lived in the area around the town of Nimbin, which is famous in Australia and around the world for its alternative culture of towns, villages, communes and collectives. I lived in the largest and most (in)famous of communes for eight years back in the '70s and '80s. It was a community that attracted some very dippy hippies. Two of my fellow communards, for example, died from snake bites because they believed they could cure themselves through meditation. Another, our neighbour, was bitten one dark night by an unidentified snake. She sought advice from the I Ching as to whether she should go to hospital or not. Having responded to a loud scream in the night, I was there with the car running, ready to take her to hospital, just in case it was one of the deadly species that frequented the area. But no, she insisted on throwing the Ching, not once, not twice but three times before she got a reading that suggested she should perhaps seek help. By this time her foot was going black and

21

she was losing consciousness. We bundled her into the car and got her to hospital just in time. She spent three days in a coma but survived.

These kinds of abuses of common sense fed my already well established scepticism. So for a long, long time, I rejected all such modes of 'reading' based on intuitive selection, such as the drawing of Tarot Cards or Runes, or the throwing of the I Ching. The drawing of Intuitive Solution cards is in essence no different to these other practices. They are all intuitive means of getting in touch with deeper, hidden levels of understanding. So my using them now indicates quite some turn around in my attitude. The change has come about as I have witnessed, time and time again here in Findhorn, the ways in which the drawing of cards can deliver such value and meaning for people, and enable them to live more inspired lives. My concern now is not whether there is scientific evidence for or against the validity of such practices. The important question is whether the process enables the protagonist to become a better person or whether it brings them more joy or helps them become a more effective change agent in the world.

So now, I draw cards myself. And I find that it works. The cards assist me to get in touch with what is going on for me at a deeper level. They do not, of course, foretell the future; they simply enable me to live a more aware and conscious life. And that in turn enables me to live more congruently with my values, which as mentioned is for me, essential to inner peace and contentment.

I will complete this chapter by describing the cards drawn for today, at time of writing. This morning I am going hiking in the Highlands with a few friends. We have had the trip planned for months. Originally, we were going for two days to the West Coast. But there's been cyclonic weather over the last few days causing widespread flooding and disruption. So we postponed the adventure by one day and shrunk our ambition; now we are going for just a day trip to a location less far. However, the weather forecast for the area remains dire – showers, high winds and very cold temperatures. So I'm feeling resistant and a touch apprehensive.

Let's see what the cards can contribute to my thinking and feeling about the matter. Before drawing them, I simply ask for a reflection on the day and my resistance to going. The first Insight card reads: *You readily appreciate and trust others.* Well, this seems clear. I am being reminded that, even though I have little experience of hiking in the mountains, there are others on the trip that do. Indeed one is a wilderness instructor and others are well experienced. So I just need in this situation to release concern, appreciate the opportunity and trust. The Setback card says: *You are afraid, through lack of faith, to let go and lose control.* Again, this has a fairly obvious interpretation. I am somewhat of a control freak. Today's hike, given the weather, is literally and figuratively way out of my comfort zone. I have little experience to fall back on. So the card suggests, much like the first one, that I need to let go and trust. The final Insight card tells me: *You live life to the fullest, enjoying each creative moment.* This is a nice reminder. I do indeed like to live life fully. The day's adventure is likely to be demanding, but being in the wild, *especially* if it's challenging, will be exhilarating. And there will be lots of personal learning available, hopefully of an inner strength and resilience that I haven't tapped in quite this way before. Creative moments? Perhaps I should take my camera. The Angel I selected was *Gratitude.* This is always a pertinent reminder, but especially today. I have unexpectedly been invited to accompany close and respected friends on an excursion into the wilds of nature. What's not to be grateful about?

There are a million combinations of cards and a myriad of interpretations I could make. These ones are quite literal and not at all deep. But that's the way the cards fell. I am heading out with more trust, excitement and gratitude than I was feeling before. And that's a good thing. I expect the trip may be the subject of a subsequent chapter. So I'd better get some pics along the way.

5

TAIZÉ

This chapter is about my most valued spiritual practice – the one that is most effective and the one I most enjoy. Every weekday morning, I step out of the house at 8 am, walk across the road, along a narrow stone pathway that winds its way through vegetation, up and over a wee mound, and delivers me to the entrance of one of the best loved and most photographed buildings in our community, the Nature Sanctuary, famous around the world for it's organic form and materials, as well as the beauty and symbolic power of its interior. This magical and sacred space that is home to one of our most well established community rituals. We call it Taizé.

Taizé is actually a monastery and community in France – 'a community where kindness of heart and simplicity [are] at the centre of everything' said Brother Roger who established the monastery shortly after WWII. Run by catholic brothers, it attracts thousands of local and international visitors every year – people from many different backgrounds and faiths. They come in good part because of the style of worship, which is based on the singing of short simple songs, repeated time and time again much like a mantra might be in meditation. Indeed, the singing of these songs *is* a meditation. This quote from their website, www.taize.fr, sums it up.

> Using just a few words they express a basic reality of faith, quickly grasped by the mind [and] sung over many times, this reality gradually penetrates the whole being. Meditative singing becomes a way of listening to God. It allows everyone to take part in a time of prayer together and to remain together in attentive waiting on God.

I find myself smiling at my choice of this quote. As I wrote in Chapter 1, I have been areligious all my life. I had an orthodox Jewish upbringing but had decided by the time I was 12 or so that the notion promulgated at Sunday School, of a single omnipotent omniscient God the creator was an invented nonsense. I have been an atheist in respect of such a God ever since. But in being at Findhorn, I have slowly released my resistance to the use of the 'G word'. Indeed I use it myself these days in reference to an entirely different kind of god – the god within – that spark of divinity that exists within us all. This conceptualisation fits with my humanistic worldview. It's shorthand, as I see it, for that potential we all have as human beings for the fullest possible expression of creativity, service and love, amongst other things.

Our community here at Findhorn is very rich in many different ways. Daily life is packed with interest. A strong aspect of that richness is our cultural life. At Findhorn, there is singing, dancing and performance of all kinds. We sing and dance spontaneously e.g the kitchen crew, which currently includes several Latins from Spain and South America, frequently dance their way through a work shift. And we sing, dance and perform more formally, for example: in Sacred Dance sessions scheduled once or twice a week; in fortnightly Open Mike sessions (impromptu performances by musicians and poets); in monthly 'Sharings' (of recitals, comedy, performances etc.); and in Taizé. Our cultural life is a key ingredient of the community glue here, along with our spirituality and ecological concerns and practices. These three strains to the culture are separate and distinct, but also blend together beautifully to help build the culture and strengthen relationships.

But, back to Taizé, which landed in Findhorn in the mid 1980s with the arrival of Barbara Swetina, a much loved community songstress and musician who has lived here ever since. She had just come from the Taizé monastery and was inspired. Another long-standing and deeply appreciated community member, Ian Turnbull had just finished building the Nature Sanctuary. Ian's sacred space seemed like a perfect match for Barbara's prayerful singing, so together, they initiated half-hour long, morning Taizé sessions that have continued in the same space until today. The sessions are facilitated by one of a dedicated group of leaders who set up the space, select the songs and lead the singing. Somewhere between ten and thirty people attend, depending on the season and the number of guests we have visiting at the time. (The two are correlated; many more guests come in summer than at other times.) Most songs are sung in three or four part harmony. So we sit grouped in our voice parts: base, tenor, alto and soprano.

We begin by sounding three OMs. This is a way of bringing ourselves present, warming up our voices and somehow preparing the ground for spirit to enter – for the participants to align with their essence, source, higher self or inner divinity (pick your own understanding). There are usually just four songs, each of which lasts about five minutes. Actually, the song itself is only a few lines long but is repeated ten or twenty times. The first song is usually a round, without voice parts but still sprightly, requiring quite some focus and concentration. This will be followed by two more songs in harmonised voice parts. These are usually slower in pace and more meditative. They are melodic, generally quite beautiful, and simple (easy to learn). The lyrics are usually in Latin but there are plenty of other songs in different languages from different religions and spiritual traditions.

After the third song, we spend a few minutes in prayer. As the leader will inevitably announce (for the benefit of newcomers), 'prayers can be spoken out loud in any language or in the silence of our hearts.' I find this a particularly precious time of sharing what's important to us, and of being reminded of the universality of being human i.e. no matter what our background, belief system, age or education, we share a commonality of: needs and wants; fears and concerns; dreams and aspirations. We usually have guests from all around the world, and mostly their prayers resonate with all of us, with the collective unconscious.

Finally, we finish with an upbeat song that sends us out into the world with a smile, and in my case with an earworm. I usually sing aloud the same song as I walk to the Main Sanctuary which is the venue for the next phase of my morning practice. And the subject of the next chapter.

I want to finish this topic on a particularly personal note, somewhat prompted by this quote that I found on the Taizé monastery website.

To open the gates of trust in God, nothing can replace the beauty of human voices united in song. This beauty can give us a glimpse of "heaven's joy on earth," as Eastern Christians put it. And an inner life begins to blossom within us.

These early chapters have been about the unfolding of my spiritual journey at Findhorn; how I arrived here 10 years ago with little space in my worldview for such concepts as God, spirit, subtle realms, and the myriad more esoteric aspects of Findhorn's history and culture. And that now, in the last few years at least, my attitudes have softened and changed. I am now much more open-hearted and open-minded. Well, I would say that Taizé has been one of the primary influences; its essence, it's core message i.e. "to open the gates of trust in God," has slowly seeped into my being. I now trust where once I would have been sceptical and suspicious.

The other way in which Taizé has been hugely personally transformative, and for which I will be eternally grateful, is this – I arrived in Findhorn convinced that I was not, and would never be, a singer. I had spent a lifetime convinced that I was tone deaf. So, even attending Taizé in the early days was challenging. But I have always loved listening to music, particularly choral singing. So I initially attended for the opportunity to listen in, and indeed, be immersed in some live, good quality, choral singing. It didn't take long for the music to weave its magic. Due simply to the nature of the songs – that they are short, simple, tuneful, repetitive and easy to remember – I started to sing along, very quietly at first.

It took me a while and quite some practice before I gained confidence, but sure enough the confidence came. And in what I perceived to be the non-judgemental atmosphere of the sessions, I started to sing louder and with more feeling. Soon I started to believe that perhaps I was able to sing in tune after all. And when I asked the experienced singers on either side of me, they assured me that indeed, I was singing in tune and furthermore, I had a strong and rich baritone singing voice. I have never looked back. These days I sing without self-consciousness. And in doing so, I completely lose myself in the music. It has become for me, a real meditation – a means by which I access inner stillness, peace of mind and openness of heart, every day. Such is the potential for personal growth and transformation in the practices we have evolved here in Findhorn.

6

GOING WITHIN

I have been slow to start this chapter because I feel completely unqualified to write on the topic. And yet, I also feel compelled to do so. 'Going within' is probably *the* most quintessential aspect of the culture here in the Findhorn Foundation and community. I feel I *have* to write about it whether or not I am willing or able. So this may end up being quite a short chapter; I have no idea how well it will flow.

I'm resistant because for most of my adult life I've been unable (and, it must be said, unwilling) to establish a meditation practice. This is despite having been surrounded by committed practitioners all my life. My mother meditated twice daily when I was a youth still living at home. For many years, she attended the School of Economic Science, also known as the School of Philosophy, a worldwide organisation based in London. Its teachings are based in *Advaita Vedanta*, a branch of Hinduism as interpreted by founder, Leon MacLaren (1910-1994). Mum and I have always been close. And she is a true inspiration in many ways – always calm, clear and loving. But she could not get me to attend an introductory course, despite many invitations to do so. The organisation and their practices seemed just too inward looking and esoteric for my taste, preoccupied as I was at the time with radical activism in the world.

One of my brothers, however, did enter the organisation. He and his family have been deeply involved in the London branch of the School for decades. My brother, too, is an inspiration – a successful professional in a very demanding field, yet a wonderfully measured man with a calm and kindly disposition. I don't think I've ever seen him angry or upset. He has meditated twice a day, every day, for the last thirty years. The woman to whom I was married for 22 years also had a strong meditation practice. I well remember her attending a ten day Theravāda Buddhist meditation retreat when our first child was just a few months old. I attended too, but as baby sitter. I spent each day cruising with my child in a beautiful rainforest setting, presenting her for feeding whenever she was hungry.

All of these people I deeply love and respect and yet I never once took their example; I never seriously attempted a meditation practice. I remained unwilling, defiant even, for reasons which I now find hard to accept myself. I guess I have regrets about that. However, after several years here in Findhorn, I have finally taken the plunge. For the last year I have attended group mediation sessions most mornings as part of my daily spiritual practice – a rhythm that I've been describing over several chapters. My day typically begins early with up to several hours of reading or writing and continues with a healthy breakfast prepared the night before. Then I draw cards, before leaving the house and crossing the road to *Taizé*, a session of prayerful singing. Finally, I proceed on foot to the Main Sanctuary, a potent space within a modest building where the community has been gathering to meditate for almost fifty years. There, we sit together in silence for 20 minutes. After that, I leave for the office where, at least on Monday mornings, but often at other times as well, I will again sit with my colleagues in silence for a few minutes before beginning work. This is what we call an *attunement*.

I have described how my being at Findhorn has progressively softened my sceptical worldview. So it has been with my resistance to meditation. For many years I didn't participate, but slowly, slowly, as my mind and heart were prised open through being immersed in the culture here, I dropped the resistance and opened to the possibility. As part of this unfolding, I was reaching a deeper level of contentment with my life generally. This helped me access a certain inner stillness which was conducive to further spiritual exploration. Nowadays, I am keen to get to Sanctuary in the morning, but I struggle with the practice. I have always spent a lot of time in my head; it's forever busy. So simply stilling the mind is a real challenge – I find it far from simple. I've utilised several techniques for doing so: focussing on the breath, repeating a mantra, counting, counting backwards etc. They all seem to work for a period but after a few days or a week seem totally unable to prevent my mind from wandering off somewhere not very useful. And I understand this is normal – that most everyone struggles with meditation in this way. At the moment I'm using visualisation as a technique. It's proving helpful. Occasionally I surprise myself with a sustained period of thoughtlessness (in the best possible way, of course) or a strong visceral sensation that rather wonderfully pulls my attention from the mind to the heart. I have come to realise too, that patience and acceptance of whatever is going on are part of the practice. It is, as they say, the "journey not the destination" that counts.

We have two regular morning meditations in the Main Sanctuary. At 6.30 the most committed brethren sit in silence for an hour together. The more popular session occurs at 8.30 and is guided i.e. someone will read a few lines of text or recite a short poem that might support or inspire those attending to take their meditation deeper. Unusually, the meditation leader recently played his didgeridoo to invoke focus on the breath. For me, the collective element is also an important dimension. Being in the stillness with up to 60 other people, in a space that's been used for the purpose for such a long time, is a powerful experience in and of itself. And I'm very much reminded as I sit there, of the core purpose of our community established by founders, Peter,

Eileen and Dorothy some fifty years ago, which is to bring about personal and planetary transformation. This is nowhere better described than on a wee plaque in the lobby of the Sanctuary, one so modest that it goes unnoticed by many who walk past it to enter, squeezed up as it is against the fire extinguisher. It carries the words of Eileen Caddy.

> Why do we need time at the sanctuary? ... It is a place where we can come together collectively to consciously generate the energies of love, light, peace, joy, wisdom and divine power, which we do in silence. Then at the end these energies can be sent out, not only to those around us or to the community alone, but to the world. This is where we become 'world servers' and link up with the 'network of light.'

A perhaps less visionary but equally vital purpose is ascribed to what we call *attunement*. The concept was first developed at Findhorn in the '70s by David Spangler, sometimes referred to as the fourth founder of our community. Attunement, he says, requires a repatterning of one's inner state so as to align or connect with spirit. It involves shifting consciousness to allow greater sensitivity and openness to subtle phenomena. In Findhorn we utilise attunement many times a day. Many of us begin a work shift with an attunement in order to bring ourselves present and to connect with colleagues. We begin almost every meeting with an attunement to enable collective alignment of purpose. We may use it in a decision-making process to gain access to a deeper truth than the facts alone reveal. We might use it to connect with particular qualities that we wish to invoke for some purpose or other. Indeed, we use it almost any time we do something of purpose.

An attunement is a mini-meditation of sorts. Someone will lead, requesting that those present close their eyes or focus on the ever present candle in the centre. (We mostly do this sitting in a circle.) Then, we might take a few deep breaths together to bring ourselves present. This helps to leave behind (mentally, emotionally and psychically) whatever has been going on for us prior. Then the facilitator will lead an appropriate blessing, invocation or visualisation, depending on the needs of the moment. Attunements vary widely and yet there is a commonality to them too. Indeed those of us who have been here a while don't really need to be led as such. We can simply close our eyes and attune together without a facilitator. The process can take between one and five minutes. I love them. And I don't find them challenging, as I would a longer meditation. There is not enough time for the mind to wander too far.

By way of illustration, in the Findhorn Foundation we typically allocate staff accommodation by this process. If a room becomes available in a staff house, an advertisement will go out seeking expressions of interest from coworkers needing a room or a change of room. At a prearranged time, those interested will meet with a facilitator and the rest of the household to discuss and attune. Firstly, each candidate will put their case – the facts of the matter – why they particularly would like to move in. This will be followed by the attunement that will involve a visualisation. The facilitator will paint with words, a picture of the building or perhaps the room in question. And then, he/she will invoke an image of each of the candidates approaching the building and entering (or not). Naturally enough, each participant will have a slightly (or dramatically) different visualisation.

The facilitator will bring a close to the inner process and solicit responses from each person present. And this is where things can get interesting. In turn, each will reveal what it was they 'saw'. Sometimes the visualisations are clear. One person might have felt that the door was locked or jammed. This will usually be enough to cause them to drop out of contention. Others might see themselves entering the space and feeling a particular emotion, positive or negative, or have some other kind of experience. Whatever the outcome, it will usually carry a prompt or a message that will enable the person to make a choice about whether to drop out of the process or continue. If more than one candidate wishes to continue then usually the process is repeated, and repeated, until a resolution is found. Occasionally, no clear outcome is reached in the allocated time and a second attunement will be called. Eventually, resolution will be reached (although on one occasion in recent years, straws were drawn after multiple failed attempts to attune). And this is where I can find myself challenged. Sometimes the outcome will appear to be quite counter intuitive, illogical or perhaps even unjust. Findhorn is a 'mystery school' they say; it's important not to be attached.

'Love in action' is our most diffuse and widely practised spiritual modality. Derived from the phrase, 'work is love in action' attributed to Peter Caddy, it's a way of being in the world whereby one brings full attention and devotion to whatever one is doing. It's about honouring and connecting with the sacred within oneself and in all things – with *oneness*. In our service departments, where guests spend several work shifts a week, the concept takes particular significance. Guests are encouraged to go within, attune, and bring all of their attention to the task at hand – to 'do it with love'. Famously, once a year when the Maintenance team are stocktaking, some lucky guest will be offered the opportunity to count the screws, with love! And so it is with everything we do here really.

For me, this is the most effective carrier of spirit. And, in a way, I think it's something I've always done; I've always been fully engaged with whatever I was doing. Bringing full attention, dedication and enthusiasm to my work has been easy. At a very young age I watched a TV series by Joseph

Campbell. I took to heart his encouragement to 'follow your bliss.' Generally, I have very poor long term recall, but I still carry a clear image of him sitting in an armchair and speaking those words directly to me, or so it seemed. Ever since, I have pro-actively fashioned my life in a way that has kept me passionate and engaged. That's meant making a radical change to my circumstances every seven or eight years – taking a different job, moving to a new country, adopting a new lifestyle etc. It seems that about seven years is what it takes for me to feel that I've learned the lessons and met the challenges available, and that I need a change if I'm to continue to learn and grow. It's somewhat of a relief, therefore, to have been at Findhorn for 10 years now and *not* developed that seven year itch. Actually, I think it took me the first seven years just to land here – to shake off my predispositions and begin to open to the new. I feel that I'm just getting started now! And that this new phase will increasingly involve 'going within' in all of the multiple ways we do that at Findhorn.

7

NATURE AND THE SUBTLE REALMS

This chapter has been written expressly for this book; it never appeared in the blog. I realise now that I had skirted the issue whilst blogging and perhaps that was ok. But it's clear that it would be extremely remiss of me to publish a book about the culture of the Findhorn Foundation and Community that does not in some way recognise the deepest held and most famous aspects of our culture – our relationship with nature and the 'subtle realms.'

I've not ever written on this topic before now because I've felt unqualified to do so. I have little personal experience of the kind of relationship with nature that many of our members enjoy. Historically, and continuously to the present day, many Findhorn community members have experienced extraordinary connection and interaction with unseen elements of the natural world and the so called subtle realms. I have little experience of such things and my somewhat sceptical, material worldview doesn't permit me to simply accept such phenomena uncritically. Yet, I have no ready explanation, so I find the matter curious and perplexing. (As an aside, I have a similar relationship with crop circles. I've researched them thoroughly and find them totally mystifying.)

Here is a case in point from just yesterday. Indeed it was this communication in the form of an email that prompted me to write this chapter. (It's included here in its entirety for completeness.)

Dear all,

NFD are preparing to dig a trench along the runway from the Earthships down to the Guest Lodge and then across the Village Green. As this will involve the cutting back of trees, shrubs and flowers, NFD have given Park Garden group time to attune to the project, to the land, the plants and animals, and to the associated angelic and elemental lives. Yesterday we assessed the likely impact, and this morning we held an attunement to inform the nature kingdoms about the project.

We affirmed the need to make the Park safer and more beautiful by burying a new electricity cable and thus being able to remove all the overhead ones, and that the planned route has been decided after consideration of all the options. We walked down the route, looking at all the plants and deciding what was best for them, and will work with NFD to minimise the impact.

In our attunement we felt gratitude from the nature kingdoms for clear communication, for conscious co-operation, and for the love and care we take in all the work. We affirmed that the project will be carried out and completed safely and efficiently.

We felt that we were doing this on behalf of the whole community, and so I am writing now to tell you that the initial energetic work of co-operation and co-creation has been done, and that the response from the nature kingdoms has been filled with gratitude and appreciation.

We invite you to hold the project in light and love as it proceeds.

With thanks to NFD for the time to do the energetic groundwork,

Angus

on behalf of Park Garden

So what am I to make of this? I am sceptical, but not cynical; I don't for a second, doubt the veracity of Angus's words nor the experience of the Park Gardens team. Yet, I'm at somewhat of a loss to know how to interpret this story. It reads as if the team communicated directly with the nature kingdom – 'to the land, the plants and animals, and to the associated angelic and elemental lives.' And it sounds as if the nature kingdom answered back. The casual reader certainly could not be blamed for assuming that the words above are literal and the intercommunication was 'real.' Did the Park Gardens team feel that? Or was there something else going on? Before I publish this chapter I'm going to run it past Angus for his feedback. I love Angus. He's one of the great stalwarts of our community and a man whom I greatly respect. I'm looking forward to unpacking the matter with him. But in the meantime, here's my take.

As previously mentioned, I believe that we human beings, individually and collectively, possess enormous untapped potential. Each of us is capable of levels of achievement that we can't even imagine, which could be unlocked if only we could identify and apply the right means. Sometimes those means are pro-active; we might take a course of learning, develop a practice, collaborate with others etc. And at other times, all that's required is that we be with what is; be open, be still, and 'listen.' This second way of being I have experienced to great effect many times, most notably on two 'mind-blowing' occasions, once in the '70s in the middle of the Sinai Dessert and the other almost 10 years ago at the Findhorn River. I think of them as the only two (non drug-induced) mystical experiences of my life.

On the first occasion I was on tour with a busload of youngsters. We had arrived at the foot of Mt Sinai in the evening and set up camp, planning to climb to the legendary Orthodox monastery, Santa Caterina, the following morning. Late that night, I went for a walk on my own in the dessert. After some time, I sat on a rock to rest. In those days I was youthfully zealous, politically rabid and philosophically opinionated – anything but open, still and able to listen. It was decades before I ever attempted meditation. And yet, in that moment, something magical occurred. I can only guess that what happened was due to the conditions in which I found myself: being in the middle of a vast, vast dessert; one that's completely arid and devoid of vegetation; where the air is as dry and clean as anywhere on Earth; on a night when the stars were as bright and as numerous as I'd ever seen in my life. Due to the context and rarefied atmosphere, I was somehow able to soften my shell, let down my defences and allow myself an experience of the infinite – of 'oneness.'

As I sat on the rock I slowly became aware of my connection with it – that the rock and I were made of the same fundamental stuff and that we were, in fact, one. My attention was then drawn to the sand around the rock and I 'saw' the same elemental interconnection between the rock on which I sat and the sand upon which it rested. So now I'm as one with both the rock and the dessert floor; we form a continuum. Soon enough my awareness expanded further to include the surrounding wadi (valley) and I now felt fully interconnected, at one, with everything up to and including the mountains all around. Slowly, gradually, my awareness and understanding expanded onward and outward to include the whole of the dessert, the region, the Earth, the stars and, ultimately, the whole damned Universe. I was as one with all that is.

I don't know how long the experience lasted, perhaps five or ten minutes, or perhaps one or two; I really have no idea. But when I came to, I was left with the unshakeable conviction that I, we, everything is fully interconnected. From that day onward I have known this as an incontrovertible truth, because (and here's the rub) I had it proven to me! I 'saw' it with my own 'eyes'. Did I literally see it? I don't know. Perhaps I did. Perhaps our visual faculties are capable of such things. But actually, I think that's irrelevant. By some means or other, I arrived at a crystal clear understanding of an essential truth that has lived in me ever since.

And again, during Experience Week, I had a similar vision, except that this time it involved a beautiful woman, a magnificent tree and my very first visit to Randolf's Leap on the Findhorn River, one of the most awe-inspiring riverscapes I have ever come across. No doubt, I was already in somewhat of an altered state, being three or four days into a programme designed to shift perceptions and dissolve defences. So on both occasions, due to circumstances, my barriers were down and 'the veils were thin,' as they say. When the veils are thin enough, it seems that even sceptical ol' me is capable of and open to unfathomable depths of perception.

Much more often, indeed regularly, I experience a less profound but nonetheless still deep and moving level of awe and wonder. It can happen if I'm looking at a beautiful painting, or standing in a fine architectural space, or listening to gorgeous music. It can happen in a natural rainforest or a well-designed garden setting. Somehow, I am transported in such moments to a place of pure bliss and deep contentment. Invariably tears flow. Again, there seems to be something going on there that causes my defences to come down and allow in a different kind of experience to what I think of as 'normal.' Perhaps it's some kind of return to innocence – layers of conditioning being peeled away to enable a state of wonder more commonly associated with early childhood.

Anyway, getting back to Angus's story – my interpretation (before having spoken to him) is that the Park Gardens team experienced something like that which I've just described. There are people, many of them, in this community who are very practiced at attunement. They can close their eyes and drop into a space where the 'veils become thin' quite readily. They can quite quickly align with the energies and/or entities that are being invoked. I'm guessing that Angus and his colleagues experienced a deep empathy with the plants and animals in question and, via a strong sense of their interconnection, were able to 'feel' or 'hear' an energetic response. And I imagine that the experience was quite different for each of them.

Angus's story illustrates the complexity of our relationship with nature here in Findhorn. We are both a spiritual community, in large part premised on our relationship with nature, and also an ecovillage. We began as just the former and adopted the latter identity in the '80s. These days, I think it's fair to say, we have a kind of a dual personality – we see ourselves and are viewed by others as either or both a spiritual community and an ecovillage. For the most part, these two aspects of our culture co-exist in harmony. It's been said that they are two sides of the one coin. But there are times when a creative tension arises between the two. I think this is well illustrated in the above account of what occurred when the NFD needed to run a trench through some of the gardens in order to progress our renewable energy infrastructure.

Another classic example of this kind of tension occurs when there's tree pruning and felling to be done. When the community began back in the '60s there were very few existing trees on the site. These days there are thousands growing throughout the ecovillage. Many of them are magnificent specimen trees. Some have grown up on the south side of community and residential buildings, thus blocking their access to sun and light. Trees of course, are much valued generally, for their intrinsic value and beauty as well as their contribution to the environment. But here in Findhorn they are considered and valued much as sentient beings. To many people in the community, removing a limb from a tree, or felling one, is tantamount to amputation or murder. Historically, we chose not to prune or fell trees just because they blocked the sun from buildings and gardens. But in the last 10 years or so, as our identity as an ecovillage has matured and we've applied more and more effort to reducing our carbon footprint, it's become increasingly obvious that something had to be done. And so we've become much more willing to prune and fell trees to this end. And yet, it's still very painful for many of our members. Hence, we almost always inform the community prior to any significant tree lopping or removal so that individuals are given the opportunity to attune and communicate (or perhaps even grieve) much as the Park Garden team did recently.

I'd like to tell one final story about another such instance of creative tension that arose when we installed a centralised biomass boiler some four or five years ago; probably the most significant infrastructure project of recent years. As designer and project manager, I had to configure the route taken by the district heating pipe, from the boiler itself to the dozen or so buildings which it fed with carbon zero heat. Many of those buildings are located in what we call the Central Garden, the very first ornamental garden that Peter Caddy designed and built in the late '60s and early '70s. All our gardens are precious of course, but the Central Garden is as a temple to us; it's a sacred space! Any damage wrought by the pipeline installation would be considered sacrilegious by some and cause considerable angst for many more. So the solution we struck was to route the requisite meter deep trench along the existing pathways through the garden, a quite circuitous and ostensibly inefficient route. By this means, almost no damage was done to the gardens. Yet the exercise was more troublesome and expensive than would have been a more direct, straight line layout. Such are the lengths we can go to appease the denizens of the subtle realms as well as the sensibility of community members.

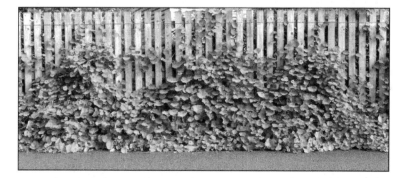

PART TWO

OUTER WORK

8

COMMUNITY MEALS

In this second section I move from the very personal world of our 'inner work' to the more social, cultural and political dimensions of community life in Findhorn – that which I've called 'outer work.' For indeed, it is work!

I have resided in several intentional communities over the last forty years (indispersed with stints in the mainstream). And I have visited dozens more, either casually or for research purposes. On the basis of this experience and my reading of the literature on communal living, I believe that shared meals are the single most important 'ritual' in the daily life of almost all intentional communities. Certainly at Findhorn, our community meals are, and have always been, central to the culture and a critical component of the social glue.

We eat together twice a day – lunch and dinner. Not all of us partake, of course. We are a community of around 700 people and typically, our kitchens each cater for about 100 people at a time, many of whom will be guests.[1] Nonetheless, it is clear to me that these meals are crucial to community life – they have a practical advantage and provide an important opportunity to engage socially. And, of course, there is something powerfully symbolic about sharing a meal, both with members of one's 'tribe' and with guests. I am no anthropologist, but I would guess that 'breaking bread' holds this value (and has forever done so) for almost every cultural group, anywhere in the world.

As a staff member of the Findhorn Foundation (FF), I receive a 'salary package' that comprises: sustenance (food and other essentials), accommodation and some cash. So for me and my fellow coworkers, there is additional meaning to our eating together – it has financial implications. And, at a symbolic level, it emblemises our common economy.[2] Personally, I deeply appreciate our shared meals for many, many reasons. I eat in the CC (Community Centre) at every opportunity, and have been doing so without change since I first arrived here ten years ago (the exceptions being when I

---

[1] We have two kitchen/dining rooms, one in each campus. The Community Centre in the Park, Findhorn, has a maximum capacity of about 180. In Cluny (our campus in Forres, five miles away) the dining room can seat about 120 people.

[2] In economic terms, the Findhorn Foundation is an income sharing, or egalitarian, subset of the community as a whole. In the Foundation, staff receive exactly the same financial remuneration irrespective of their contribution (job). It's a demonstration of the essential socialist principle, from each according to his ability, to each according to his needs! I cherish the principle and the practice; it's one of the reasons I came to Findhorn and joined the Foundation.

choose to eat at home with a friend or partner).

Having lunch and dinner provided (at 12:30 and 6:00 pm) has, for me, immense practical advantage. It saves me a *lot* of time: I don't need to shop for ingredients; nor spend time preparing the meal; and, I don't need to clean up afterwards or even wash my own dishes. So, our meal system creates tremendous spaciousness in my life, which contributes significantly to an absence of stress. Common meals are an important opportunity to catch up socially with friends and colleagues – to share conversation and deepen our connection with each other. And, for better or worse, they are an important opportunity to discuss business.

The food we serve is vegetarian (although not always, and I'll come back to that). The ingredients are, as much as we can make them, fresh, organic, local and seasonal. And the food is prepared with love – the kitchen crews demonstrate our key ethos, *work is love in action*, every single shift. In my opinion, food served in the CC and in Cluny is of a very high quality given that it's prepared for large numbers of diners. It is, I believe, truly delightful – it delights *all* of the five senses.

It would be remiss of me if, in this homage to shared meals, I ignored the commercial dimension to all this. The FF is famous as a spiritual organisation, but it is also a business. We are an educational charity and our income is mostly derived from the fees our guests pay to attend our workshops, conferences and events. So, providing sustenance for our guests is an underlying and crucial value to the meal system. This factor affects the nature of the meals; it's a key reason for maintaining such high quality. There is a tradition, and an ethos, of ensuring that guests delight in the food we serve. We know how important food is to most people and how much it can influence our visitors' overall experience. I think it behoves the rest of us who partake of these meals, FF coworkers and other community members, to appreciate that common meals in most other communities are generally much less exotic – much simpler and with less variety and choice.

We serve ourselves, buffet style, from a long table laden with a selection of hot and cold dishes, enabling each person to take exactly what appeals to them and/or suits their dietary needs. The cooks always prepare special alternative dishes for those people on refined diets: vegan, dairy free, sugar free, garlic free, gluten free etc. It fills me with pride in my community to be reminded at every meal, just how much trouble we take to cater for diversity, meet the needs of every individual, and in this way, demonstrate inclusivity and caring for each other.

Before the meal, we queue. Sometimes the line can be very long. I am amongst those who have a certain resistance to queuing. So I tend to arrive about ten minutes early for meals in order to stand near the top of the queue. This also provides an opportunity to check in with particular friends and colleagues over personal and business related matters. It's somewhat of a standing joke that several of the same people populate the top of the queue at every meal.

The kitchen crews are very skilled at ensuring the food is served on time. A typical cooking shift is three hours long, and yet 95% of the time, the food will be ready within minutes of the designated meal time. And occasionally, it's a little late, which is also fine; we just chat amongst ourselves until it's ready.

Dining in our community is always preceded by a

blessing. We link hands in a circle around the tables of food and the *focaliser* (coordinator) of the cooking shift will say a few words, including: a short welcome and description of the meal; followed by an invitation to close our eyes (or not, as we like); and, an expression of gratitude to 'all those beings, seen and unseen, who have helped to bring this food to our table.' This is a reference to the worms and micro-life in the soil, the food growers and transporters, and the cooks themselves. And in the tradition of this place, the 'unseen' is a reference to the devas, nature spirits and angelic forces with whom we co-create.

Then, we enjoy! At lunch there will always be a soup and a range of hot dishes and salads. At dinner there is no soup, but occasionally there'll be a desert, always on Friday nights but also on other occasions, such as last night when cake was served in honour of the birthday of our revered late founder, Eileen Caddy. The only variation to the daily regime occurs on Sunday when brunch is served at 11am. This too, will include a desert. We love our deserts!

The dining area offers a range of options for dining with one or more people. There are several tables for two or three diners but mostly we eat at tables for between 6 and 12. For larger numbers, we combine tables. On birthdays, for example, 20 or 30 people will sit at a single long table. And for such occasions, the kitchen crew will bake a cake. In summer, diners spill out onto the outdoor terrace and the grass beyond.

At the end of the meal, we deposit our dirty dishes and cutlery in a corner of the CC where they are taken care of by a KP crew. (KP stands variously for Kitchen Patrol, Kitchen Party and Karma Points!) These are the four to six people who wash dishes for everyone else. All those who eat regularly in the CC are assigned to a KP rota. In my case, I wash dishes every Thursday night. And because it's the only time during the week when I do so, I really enjoy it. It's an opportunity to serve and to feel part of a team working collectively on a crucial aspect of the day-to-day logistics of community life. The shift usually takes about an hour.

I mentioned that our meals are vegetarian but for a few exceptions. We serve meat on at least two occasions every year. These are long-standing traditions established by our founders in the very early days of the first community celebrations. We serve turkey at Xmas and also haggis on Burns night (January 25th). I suspect that some of the more committed vegetarians find these occasions challenging. And perhaps the most steadfast opt to eat at home instead. There are also occasions on which fish is served at community meals. In fact, in Cluny this is a regular occurrence. In the Park, it's rare. But such an occasion has just occurred. A few days ago, we were served with a superb Japanese meal that included sushi, some of which contained salmon. Of course there was a vegan (fish free) alternative.

My friend, Nalinii, is a new member of the regular Park kitchen cooking crew and an aspiring member of this community. She is a strongly committed vegan. Actually she has been following an even more strict, Ayurvedic, dietary regime for some years; she doesn't eat onions, garlic or mushrooms. As her contribution to the making of the meal, Nalinii created the alternative, fish free, sushi; she was not involved in preparing the fish. After the meal she was feeling pain and anger but didn't really know why. The cause surfaced a day or two afterwards, and it was about values – hers and those of the community. Nalinii believes that humans have no right to take the life of other sentient beings for our own purposes or pleasure. She felt that including fish in the meal was incongruent with the community's values of co-creation with nature. And particularly because she is new in the community, and hoping to make Findhorn her home, this incident really rocked her.

Nalinii was able to process her upset with the aid of a sharing circle of her peer group. This is one of our principle social technologies at Findhorn. Almost all of our programmes provide opportunities for participants to share what's going on for them emotionally. For many, perhaps most of our guests, this becomes the highlight of their visit – simply having the full, undivided, compassionate and non-judgemental attention of a circle of their peers. Anyway, Nalinii was able to shift at least some of the resistance, frustration and disappointment she was feeling via this process and, as we say, by doing some 'inner work.'

The episode reminded me of the challenges we face as a fully open and diverse community. At Findhorn, we accept anyone and everyone into the community, no matter what their religion or their belief system (assuming, of course, that their views and practices are not anti-social or criminal). This is both our greatest advantage (because it brings variety) and our biggest challenge, (it can cause disharmony). But, if I may speak for the community, we would not have it any other way. In my opinion, it's what makes being in our community such a joy on a minute-to-minute and day-to-day, basis. It delivers a much cherished richness to our social and cultural life.

As the focaliser might say, "Blessings on the food, on our community, and on all beings!"

9

DANCE

I've just returned home after dancing *5Rhythms* in the Universal Hall with about fifty other sweaty Findhornians of all ages. I'm feeling inspired and energised, so much so that I've decided to write this chapter about dance in our community.

We're a community that loves to dance and 5Rhythms is just one of the many forms we enjoy in regular sessions, classes and workshops. Others include: Open Floor, Sacred Dance, Céilidh and Biodanza. And there are at least three other dance forms I can think of (Ecstatic Dance, Belly Dancing and Contact Improvisation) that periodically beguile us here in Findhorn. All of these forms are celebrations of life, love and the joy of being human. Every few weeks, we hold a dance party in our Community Centre which has an excellent new sound system and mood lighting. And of course, there's dancing at private parties as well. Finally, we boast a resident dance company, *Bodysurf Scotland*, which has delivered dance activities, performances, workshops and events for over ten years. Based in the Universal Hall, their vision is to be an international centre for dance in Scotland. Findhorn is undoubtedly a haven for those who like to dance. By way of illustration, the calendar in this week's Rainbow Bridge, our community newsletter, reveals formal opportunities to dance on at least seven occasions:

Thu 11: 7.30 pm, Open Floor Movement
Sun 13: 9.30 am, Sacred Dance; 7 pm, 5Rhythms
Tues 16: 7.30 pm, Shakti Spirit Dance for Women
Wed 17: 7 pm, Sacred Dance
Fri 19: 8 pm, Ceilidh
Sat 20: 7.45 pm, James's Dancing Scottish

My personal journey with dance is not dissimilar to the one I've had with singing (which I wrote about in Chapter 5). I've spent most of my life convinced that I was irredeemably poorly coordinated and feeling awkward and self conscious when dancing. But Findhorn has cured me! It's taken a while, but over the years as I've slowly been drawn into the culture and the social milieu here, I've relaxed and opened to the joys of dancing. I believe that my journey of personal growth is, in good part, due to the high quality of our social relationships, which are generally loving, trusting and non-judgemental. In an atmosphere of trust amongst close friends, such as I experienced in the Hall tonight, self-consciousness goes away, leaving one fearless and free to explore and push one's edges i.e. self-imposed limitations. Tonight, my dancing was truly joyful and liberated in a way that just five years ago, I would not have imagined possible.

5Rhythms was first developed by New York's Gabrielle Roth in the 1970s. She drew on mystical, shamanist and indigenous sources as well as transpersonal psychology, particularly Gestalt. Lasting between one and two hours, the 5Rhythm 'wave,' as it's called, comprises five different phases (rhythms) in strict sequence: Flowing, Staccato, Chaos, Lyrical, and Stillness. The dancers are guided by changing musical moods orchestrated by a certified teacher. This evening's playlist had a distinctly Scottish flavour. But this is unusual; generally there are no such overtones. Rather, the music is interpreted by each dancer in a highly personal way, 'opening them to a new sense of freedom and possibility that is both surprising and healing, exhilarating as well as deeply restorative.' (From the 5R website.) 5Rhythms is said to be a meditation, such that body movement is used to still the mind. And tonight I really had a glimpse of that. I danced with abandon, free from self-consciousness. As the saying goes, I danced 'as if nobody was watching'.

In the last few months we have enjoyed a new dance form in the community. Called, *Open Floor*, it is a derivative of 5Rhythms that has emerged since the death of Gabrielle Roth two years ago. Apparently, in what seems to have been a chaotic succession process, several long-term 5Rhythms trainers who worked closely with Roth fell out with the organisation. It has to be said that Roth kept a very tight control on her intellectual property and the manner in which 5Rhythms was taught, promoted and spread around the world. The disaffected trainers established Open Floor as an alternative dance form and are administering its development and promulgation in a quite different manner. They use sociocracy to ensure a flat management structure and democratic decision-making process. Furthermore, Open

Floor is held under *Creative Commons* licence, ensuring that it will spread and flourish free from control. I haven't yet danced a session of Open Floor so am not going to describe it here. However, I understand that, like 5Rhythms, it invites embodiment of whatever is going on for the dancer: feelings, emotions, thoughts and passions. And that through the process, comes healing and liberation.

Sacred Dance has been closely associated with Findhorn ever since Hungarian, Bernhard Wosien, introduced it to our community in the 1970s. He was a professional dancer and professor of dance who collected traditional circle (folk) dances from throughout Europe, seeking to preserve traditions that were being lost. At Findhorn we recognised the spiritual dimension of these dances and the practice took hold. It has been a strong feature of the culture ever since. We typically hold one or two sessions per week and include a taste of Sacred Dance in our introductory, Experience Week programme. I can still vividly recall the Sacred Dance session in my Experience Week some 10 years ago. We had our eyes closed for the final dance to extremely slow meditative music (Pachelbel's Canon, I think), starting in a widespread circle but magically ending up in a tightly clustered clump in the centre of the room. The feeling of oneness, of connection with others, stayed with me for days. The experience was a revelation, especially given that the last time I had done any folk dancing was as a very reluctant primary school pupil. I hated it back then; I enjoy it immensely now. I generally enjoy Sacred Dance once a week during Sunday Taizé, which begins with one or two circle dances of a particular type. Known as Dances of Universal Peace, these are Sufi in origin, danced at a very slow meditative pace. They involve singing or chanting by the participants and invariably induce strong feelings of connectedness and group harmony, joy and peace. I also make a point of participating in our annual Festival of Sacred Dance. These week long events attract dedicated dancers from around the world, some of whom have been coming regularly since the '70s.

Céilidh, traditional Scottish dancing, is the third dance type that occurs regularly at Findhorn. The term, céilidh, is derived from the Old Irish, *céle,* meaning companion. It's a traditional social gathering, common amongst Gaelic-speaking peoples of Ireland, Scotland and parts of England. Céilidh is an essential part of the community glue of these cultures. Traditionally, guests would play music and recite songs, stories and poetry. Sometimes they would dance. This style of event continues in some areas but in recent decades, dancing has predominated. Céilidhs are traditionally held in a community hall and occasionally on a smaller scale in houses and pubs. The music, if live, is usually provided by the likes of pipes, fiddle, flute, accordion and drums. The music is cheerful and lively, as are the dances. The basic dance steps can be learned easily; instructions are provided for the uninitiated before the start of each dance. Here at Findhorn, céilidhs are taught regularly and held on special occasions (such as weddings and festivals) and at the conclusion of conferences, courses and other events. They're an opportunity for guests to learn something of our Gaelic culture and for all attending to enjoy a congenial social gathering with old and newfound friends.

I'd like to hand the last word on dance at Findhorn to my delightful neighbour, Anna Barton, a long-time resident who's been one of the forces behind Sacred Dance here. These words were written about Sacred Dance but I think they equally apply to the entire gamut of dance offerings here in Findhorn. She writes:

> At Findhorn, the purpose is to enjoy dancing together in a totally non-competitive way, to learn that it is possible for everyone to dance together, young and old alike, to feel self confident in a group that is supportive rather than critical and to be able to feel in contact with the earth, spirit and each other through the different qualities of each dance. It is also used as a tool to channel a healing energy for the dancers and for the rest of the planet.

10

WHAT I MISS ABOUT FINDHORN

I have just returned to my community after six weeks away with family in Australia. I always find it valuable to get away from Findhorn for a period. It provides an opportunity to reflect on my life there and my reasons for remaining, given that it's on the opposite side of the world from family, which includes my aging mother whose health is not good, two daughters whom I adore and their beautiful families as well as several siblings. My two grandchildren, Gus and Mattie are two years and nine months old, respectively. Separation from family is the greatest challenge, indeed the only real challenge I face in living permanently in Scotland. In every other respect, I am deeply happy in the Findhorn Foundation and community and also as a Scottish and European resident.

Over the Christmas (2014) period I stayed with both my mother on Australia's Gold Coast, and my daughter, Anna and her family who were also hosting my other daughter, Liberty and her family. They live about an hour's drive south in a beautiful rainforest setting near a town called Mullumbimby. It was a busy time for me, driving back and forth several times, living out of a suitcase, connecting and reconnecting. And whilst I was ostensibly on holiday, my various projects also required attention, sometimes for several hours a day. I did find time, however, to reflect upon and appreciate all of the gifts I have in my life at Findhorn. On one hand, I used the opportunity to step back and gain some objectivity and perspective. On the other, I couldn't help but feel deep love and appreciation for life in my adopted home. I found myself missing the community deeply. And here's why…

There are three main aspects that I most appreciate about my life in Findhorn: the people, the place and the culture. By far the most important is the people, or more specifically, my relationships with them. The place and the culture, to my mind, provide the context for those relationships. The Findhorn community is estimated to have about six or seven hundred members, although nobody really knows exactly how many; we have never conducted a census, as far as I know. I would have some form of relationship with only a small proportion of them: perhaps a little over 100, a figure approaching Dunbar's number. Dunbar is an anthropologist who argues, based on his research of primates, that the human brain can comfortably maintain only about 150 meaningful relationships.

Those 100+ community members I know by name and I know something of their background and role in the community. But more importantly, and this is the defining characteristic of such relationships, I would say, we would have a '*heart* connection.' This, for me, is what determines a significant or meaningful relationship. We would have had at least one, probably several, *heart to heart* conversations. Every time we'd meet, we would enjoy a lingering *heartfelt* hug and a meaningful exchange. Because we're a geographically defined community, I meet some of these people several times every day, so opportunities for a meeting of hearts occur frequently – too often it feels at times when there's work to be done. This results in a deeply embodied experience of what I can only describe as a 'field of love.' It feels as if I'm immersed in a culture where love is freely, constantly and generously expressed. The open-heartedness of my relationships with so many people is without doubt my primary motivation for living at Findhorn.

Such relationships will have been formed over time and mostly as a result of the very many opportunities (formal and informal) for building this kind of relationship. I'm an introvert, so relationship building doesn't come naturally to me. Opportunities for deepening connection occur formally in all manner of courses, meetings, celebrations and cultural events – in fact just about every time two or more gather together for some kind of purpose. Gatherings of all kinds usually begin with an attunement, to bring people present and induce greater alignment of purpose. Then, we often proceed with an 'ice-breaker' to help those participating loosen their defences and open their minds and hearts. These are playful activities that appeal to our inner child. Fun and laughter are excellent means of dissolving personal boundaries and enabling connection.

Depending on the nature of the gathering, further processes may be introduced to encourage a deeper experience and appreciation of 'the other.' Dancing, singing and playing what we call Discovery Games, are commonly used vehicles for deepening connection. We often include a 'sharing' whereby participants express what is going on for them, outwardly or emotionally or both. Each person in turn takes a minute or two (often longer) to convey what's currently going on in their 'private' life. The rest of the group listens attentively – with empathy and without judgement. This is probably the most direct and powerful means we have of building love and acceptance within a group setting. In the process, growth, healing and transformation commonly occur.

I have heard many a guest to Findhorn say after such an experience that they felt 'heard' for the first time in their life. By this they mean far more than just being heard aurally. Rather, they have felt accepted and appreciated (loved, even) for who and what they are. This can be a primary catalyst for healing, which can also come to those who listen when they realise that they're not alone in their innermost thoughts and feelings, that their issues are universally held by all of us. I personally believe in transparency for the sake of it. The more we humans can fully share with each other what is going on for us 'privately,' then the greater can be our individual and collective healing and transformation.

Informal opportunities for deepening connection are also numerous. Because we live, work and play together, we are constantly interacting in different settings, for a range of diverse purposes. We get to know each other in different guises. Our understanding of each other grows rich and our relationships become more authentic. It becomes impossible to 'fake it.' So generally, people don't bother; they are themselves. This is such a different way of being in the world to that which I experience elsewhere. Particularly in the conventional mainstream workplace, relationships are built around hierarchical roles and responsibilities. In the absence of awareness, they are likely to become fixed and immutable, with little opportunity for deepening. I see friends in the city meeting by appointment for a single prescribed activity. Even when they meet for recreation, their interaction is circumscribed by activity and lifestyle. Certainly this is the case in Australia. When 'the boys' enjoy a round of golf together, or families a picnic, they will typically spend precious little time consciously deepening their connection.

As mentioned, other aspects of my life in Findhorn that I most miss when I'm away include the location itself and the community culture. We live here on an isthmus – a roughly two mile long peninsular that separates Findhorn Bay from the North Sea. We are surrounded by water; the nearby beach is magnificent. There are traditional fishing villages, extensive forests and rolling countryside all within close proximity. And the Highlands, with their magnificent peaks and countless lakes and lochs, are but an hour's drive away. At Findhorn we are truly blessed by the richness and diversity of our surroundings. I love living in this location! And, to the surprise of my Australian friends, I don't even mind the weather. In fact, I think I prefer it to the steamy sub-tropical conditions I experienced recently in Australia. One can at least dress for the cold; there is little one can do (apart from resorting to air-conditioning) to alleviate extreme heat and humidity.

And, what of the community culture? I am not going to attempt to elaborate on that here. There is too much to tell. Perhaps I could offer a glimpse simply by describing my choices for this weekend. On Friday night I enjoyed our end-of-week celebratory meal with friends in the Community Centre (CC) and followed that up with a hot tub under the stars, surrounded by snow. Yesterday, I spent the morning writing the above, lunched in the CC, and met a friend afterwards for a run on the beach followed by a massage exchange. In the evening, I shared an excellent pizza from our on-site pizzeria with another friend and then went with her to watch our annual pantomime at Cluny Hill, our second campus in the town of Forres, 5 miles away. The panto was written and performed by people I know and love. It was amateur, exuberant, chaotic and hugely successful. The enormous dining room at Cluny was packed with an engaged and highly appreciative audience.

This morning (Sunday) I may play golf with friends if the weather is conducive. Otherwise I'll go to our regular Sunday morning *Taizé* session of devotional dancing and singing. Brunch will follow, providing another opportunity to catch up with friends and colleagues. I don't yet have a plan for the afternoon, but expect that something will crop up. There is almost certainly a talk scheduled for 12.30, our 'Sunday Slot,' which I'll attend if the topic is of interest. Otherwise I may just get some work done around the house. I need to chop and bring in firewood, for example. This evening I have a choice between attending a session of dance in the Hall (5Rythms) or joining a support group of friends who are exploring issues of love and sexuality. I'll probably choose the latter; the 'Healing Love and Sexuality, Findhorn' group is a new and nascent initiative that deserves support.

That is a typical weekend! The cultural life here in

Findhorn is as full and rich as I wish it to be. Most activities occur on campus. When I need a car for a short journey (to Cluny or to play golf) I can chose from the several late model vehicles (including two fully electric Nissan Leafs) in our community carpool.

Life in this community is good! I miss it when I'm away

11

RELATIONSHIPS

Having broached the matter of relationships in the last chapter, I'd like to explore the notion a bit more analytically in this one, beginning with a quick look at the etymology of the word, community. The word is derived, in part, from the Latin, *communitas*, meaning 'fellowship'. So community is, by definition, about the bonds and ties between members of a given communal group. It's about their relationships. This is the nub of community life whether it be within an *intentional* community (e.g. ecovillage, commune, kibbutz, monastery, cohousing etc) or in society at large. Additional etymological roots come from French (*comunité*, meaning 'commonness') and again, from Latin (*communis*, meaning 'shared by all or many'). So, holding in common or sharing, whether it be of land and infrastructure or values and agreements, is also fundamental to community. These two aspects, *relationships* and *sharing* are essentially what define community. In this chapter I'll focus on social relationships and discuss sharing in a later one.

In the seminal book, Habits of the Heart, Robert Bellah et. al. characterise 'classic' social relationships as those with three principal dimensions; practical, social, and moral. The authors suggest that in contemporary Western society, the practical and moral aspects have largely been suppressed. Practical and moral support, they argue, 'made sense more readily in the small face-to-face communities that characterised early American society.' Yet, it is exactly Bellah's tripartite social relationships that pervade here at Findhorn. Practical support occurs in countless ways. There's willingness to care for a neighbour's garden or feed their cat whilst they're away. Ready advice is given, and time spent, helping others to install new software or move heavy furniture. Such mutual aid can save money, alleviate stress and imbue relationships with substance. It is an essential ingredient of the 'social glue' of our community.

Social support, another constituent of Bellah's 'classic' relationships, is also pervasive here. Whilst most community members have intimate relationships with one or a few unrelated others with whom they can share personal problems, we recognise that not all members are so connected. 'Sharing' as we call it, of what is going for one personally, is quintessential to Findhorn's culture. We begin most of our meetings with a quick 'check in,' where we share how we're feeling in order that others may understand and perhaps respond with what's needed. 'Sharing' builds empathy and an awareness of, and concern for, the needs of others. For deeper levels of sharing, men's and women's support groups are common, as are all kinds of other special interest groups. Social support can be critically important in times of challenge (loss, trauma or dire need). Radically changed circumstance and emergency situations are often the catalyst for community wide support: financial challenge may enable loans to be made from an emergency support fund; a cooking roster may be developed to provide meals for a family in need; a rota may be established to care for an elderly or dying community member.

Finally, Bellah's third component, moral support, is also well in evidence here in Findhorn. I see it as support for difference, or that which is offered to minorities within the community. Gay and lesbian singles and couples, for example, are genuinely welcomed and seamlessly integrated into the community. For decades, we have held courses designed especially for the LGBT community. We also provide courses for folk with special needs. And we are cognisant of the challenges facing those members with little financial security. In recent years we have been able to build or purchase a limited number of flats for members without capital and on low income. I believe that moral support for minority and marginalised groups is a hallmark of a civilised society and I think we do that pretty well here in Findhorn. And of course, we could do more.

We could, for example, implement a pension scheme. We have none; never have, I guess because in the early days it was assumed that visitors would stay for just a limited time. In recent decades, members have been much more inclined to stay indefinitely. Some of us are 'locked in' in a financial sense, without the funds to begin a new life elsewhere. And yet, we still don't support folk in their dotage (unless they have been members for 25 years, I think the rule is).

I want to move now to interpersonal relationships – those between individual members of the community who have, lets say, been here for a period of time. I have always said, informally and in presentations, that I believe our relationships to be of a very high quality. Indeed I would say, they are the single biggest reason for my being so contented here and the main reason for my staying on (as it is, on the opposite side of the world from my much loved family, which includes: an aging mother, two daughters and their partners, young grandchildren and several siblings).

My friend Anna, an anthropologist here to 'study' us as a fully immersed participant observer, writes:

> [At Findhorn there is] a radical focus on making direct, voluntary and collaborative relationships the basis for social order. …these relationships are intentionally established and carefully managed with the aim to make them trusting, inclusive, equal and transparent.

I would go even further in my effusiveness. I experience the relationships we enjoy here as authentic, open-hearted and kind. And yes, they are also honest, such that we are not reticent or shy when direct and blunt feedback is warranted. This too is a well established cultural norm. I'm not sure if Anna would agree but I would argue that all these qualities have come to the culture as a direct consequence of the sustained application over five decades of our two core spiritual principles: open-heartedness and consciousness. If we humans interrelate thoughtfully and with an open heart, then magic happens: defences are dropped, aggression melts away and space opens for compassion, empathy and love to flow. This is the 'magic of Findhorn' as far as I'm concerned.

So finally, what of romantic or sexual relationships? And why is it such an edgy topic? Why do we not openly talk about the sexual dimension to our lives except with a few very close confidants (if we are even so lucky). I wish it were otherwise. I wonder why we struggle to make transparent something that is so important to our wellbeing. I would speculate that this has something to do with our insecurity around intimate relationships – that we feel that if we were to expose and reveal our true selves, our deepest desires, wants and needs – that this would jeopardise our hard won but illusionary sense of security, our belief that our relationships are strong, enduring and forever. Perhaps the fears go even deeper than that, to our sense of who we are and our survival instinct. Anyway, there's more on this topic in the next chapter.

I'm not cynical about love. On the contrary, I'm essentially a romantic at heart. And I realise that there are couples in perfectly happy, stable and enduring relationships. But this is not the norm here, nor elsewhere, nowadays. It seems that most of us struggle with our relationships. They come and go, not lasting very long and not fulfilling our imagined needs and wants. More and more of us, whether it be in community or in wider society, live as singles. And here in Findhorn, things are no different. Paradoxically, loneliness can be acute even in a community like ours.

For the past 15 years, I've done quite some 'research' into alternatives to the serial monogamy that seems to be the norm in our society and in most intentional communities I know. The two communities from which I've taken most inspiration are *ZEGG* and Tamera (in Germany and Portugal respectively). I visited them both several times between 2001 and 2006. Indeed, at the time, I was considering living in one or the other in preference to coming to Findhorn. These are both communities that apply the theory and live the practice of what they call 'liberated love' i.e. non-exclusive sexual relationships or polyamoury.

At both of these communities, there is the same emphasis as we have here placed on the consciousness and open-heartedness of relationships. But the difference there is what follows as a consequence. For example, at Findhorn heart-felt hugging is a norm. It's a ubiquitous form of greeting and means of expressing affection. Yet the boundary between a friendly, even sensuous, hug and one with sexual implication is very clearly held. At ZEGG and Tamera, however, any two people who feel sexual attraction, irrespective of their other relationships, are given permission (indeed, encouraged) to act on that impulse. So long as the attraction is mutual and there is no coercion, then there is community and cultural support for those two people, who could be complete strangers, to engage sexually.

I have put this rather simplistically, even crudely. Of course there is much, much more to tell. These communities have been running this research experiment into a new way of relating for some forty years. There is a mountain of thinking, writing and testing that lies behind their lifestyle. All I know is that what they do, they do with considerable wisdom, grace and style. And they see it as world work – contributing to healing the ages-old rift between the masculine and the feminine. It's my experience that they have what we have by way of authentic, trusting and loving relationships, and then some. The quality of their relating is very, very impressive.

Anyway, I have been greatly influenced by my positive experience of these two communities and their culture. I have enjoyed several ZEGG style polyamourous relationships over the last 13 years. I use the word 'enjoyed' with purpose. These relationships have been very successful, affirming and healing. And in recent years, I've privately continued the practice here at Findhorn, even though it's far from the norm here. However the time now seems right for a 'coming out' of sorts. There are a number of us here now with similar experiences and interests in alternative ways of expressing and embodying love, sex and intimacy. Many of our community have visited our sister communities, ZEGG and Tamera, and been influenced as I have. Some of us have birthed a new support group for those people who want to explore these issues; it's called 'Healing Love and Sexuality, Findhorn' (HLSF) but we generally call it the 'Intimacy Group'. We have been meeting weekly or fortnightly for the last six months. Intimate relationships are being reconsidered, discussed and researched. It's happening. The prospects are good.

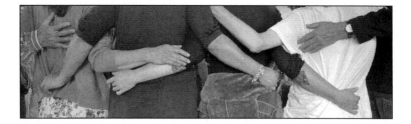

12

SEX IN COMMUNITY

It seems that sexuality is a hot topic in our community right now. But let's face it, when is it ever not? (One well-known study showed that, on average, men think about sex 34 times a day and women, 19 times.) Yet we don't seem to discuss it much. Why is that? Why is it such an edgy subject? Why do we find open discussion of the topic, in community and more generally, so challenging – threatening even?

These are exactly the questions that were the genesis of the HLSF support group. Sexuality is important to us all. We are hard wired for sexual desire in order that our species is perpetuated. Indeed all life is driven to procreate. Life begets life. Humans, of course, have (almost) uniquely evolved to be able to separate sex and procreation. (I say *almost* uniquely because Bonobo monkeys and I believe a few other species also recreate sexually.) And yet, despite sexuality being the life force of our species and central to our wellbeing as individuals, we struggle to talk about it. And I would suggest, even more so within the context of community. We struggle to talk about it and we struggle to express it, even privately, let alone publicly. I'm not going to enter into a cultural analysis of the reasons for this here. I'm not qualified. I think it's clear however, even without substantiation, that sexual thoughts, feelings and behaviours are repressed and sublimated in our Western, post-Victorian, middle class culture, and most elsewhere as well. And most of us are frustrated, unfulfilled and/or damaged as a result.

Our HLSF group has arisen from the deep need that most of us carry to heal the wounds this creeping catastrophe has caused. Our meetings provide an outlet and a forum for the expression of long suppressed thoughts, feelings and behaviours. Recent meetings have been truly liberating. In the last few weeks I have witnessed some deep and courageous sharing from participants as they open wounds (that they've been carrying for a lifetime in many cases) in order that healing and transformation may begin. This has been particularly inspiring for me as someone who so strongly believes in the value of transparency.

To that end, I published a book in 2014 titled, 'Deepening Love Sex and Intimacy: A True Story' about a relationship that I enjoyed in that year. It is not just about the joys of relationship (as the title might suggest). It's as much, if not more, about the challenges. The feedback I've received has been very positive. It's repeatedly focussed on the openness of the sharing and how inspired and comforted readers have been in realising that they are not alone with their interpersonal challenges. Knowing we are not alone can be a catalyst for healing and transformation. I passionately believe that the more we humans can fully share what's going on for us at a deep level, the greater can be our individual and collective healing and transformation. This was our main motivation, my ex-lover and I, for publishing the book.

The book is very revealing in many ways of both myself and my ex (who currently still lives in the community). It exposes our less than flattering behavioural patterns and vulnerabilities. The book also contains passages that are quite sexuality explicit. So I'm surprised and relieved that there's been no backlash, or even much negative feedback, from my community. And this, I think, approaches the issue I most wanted to breach with this chapter. The Findhorn Foundation and Community (to use our full title), like most intentional communities is, in many ways very conservative. With a few exceptions, members have come from conventional middle class backgrounds. And of course, they have brought their conventional middle class values with them. Without an overt ideology which seeks to challenge, counter or overturn those values, our community perpetrates the norms we have inherited. That's to be expected. However, not all intentional communities are like that. There have been many historically, e.g. the famous Oneida (1848-1880), and there are numerous contemporary groups that deliberately seek to overturn inherited values and behaviours and develop an alternative, more radical, set of sexual norms.

My first experience of the challenge faced by intentional communities in dealing with sexual matters was very painful. It happened when I was a youthful, somewhat naive, 22 year old living on kibbutz in Israel. This was my first experience of intentional community life. I had gone to Israel specifically to live on kibbutz. Since my mid-teens, I had been a committed, card carrying socialist (and have been ever since). At the time, Kibbutz was considered one of the most successful and radical communal experiments anywhere in the Western world. And because I was Jewish I was able to enter and live in Israel indefinitely. I was so convinced that kibbutz life was going to suit me that I officially emigrated from Australia. And so it proved. I absolutely fell in love with the lifestyle. It suited me to a tee. Unfortunately, as it turned out, I also fell in love with a married woman. We enjoyed a passionate, clandestine affair for a few months before being outed. And shortly thereafter, without ceremony or even due consideration, I was 'invited' to leave the kibbutz. This felt totally unjust to me as it was common knowledge that extramarital affairs were commonplace amongst members. It was almost the norm. But I was made a scapegoat because I had relatively recently arrived and was not yet a full member. I was expendable. I believe that, in good part, I was expelled because our affair threw light on the dark. It exposed the underbelly of dishonest sexuality that was enjoyed but not acknowledged by many of the kibbutz establishment. Perhaps it was through this experience that my commitment to transparency first developed. I left Israel eventually, not because of this incident but because I didn't fancy joining their army and fighting wars. And I've been seeking a kibbutz-like lifestyle ever since. This is probably why I am so content in Findhorn. In terms of lifestyle, I believe that our community is about the closest thing to kibbutz outside of Israel. But I digress.

I love my community, and I'm proud of what has been achieved here over decades of social evolution. For the most part, I resonate with our established values and norms. I love, for example, that we welcome and support of gay and lesbian couples. There are many living here. Ironically, I think that in some ways we are more comfortable with homosexuality than heterosexuality. We regularly run courses for the LBGT community but we haven't, in the ten years I've been here, held too many sex related programmes for straights – Tantra, for example. Anything that's at all edgy in that way is shuffled off to our sister community, Newbold House, some 6 miles away. I'll be commuting to and from Newbold for a Tantra programme I'm attending in a few weeks. Why is that? Why is there such sensitivity to expressions of overt sexuality within the community? One reason, I believe, is its potential for negative impact on our image. There have been times in the past when the Findhorn community has copped some quite harmful press. And because the Findhorn Foundation, the key organisation, is dependent on positive publicity for its survival as an educational charity, it's understandably sensitive to how we are portrayed in the media. Concern about the potential for bad publicity is definitely a reason.

But I think there's more to it than that. And it's in part to do with the norms and values we have inherited. Peter and Eileen Caddy were radical in many ways, but they were also very, very English. Peter was a career military officer who wore a stiff upper lip to suit. And whilst, by all accounts, the community demographic in the '70s was representative of the libertine climate of those times, many of the most radical members left in the early '80s when the economic going got tough (we came close to bankruptcy). A period of consolidation ensued and a more conservative milieu was established. The membership self-selected accordingly. And I think that we still carry that inherent pragmatic conservatism today. There's at least one more reason why sex talk doesn't receive much air time here. It's not acknowledged by our spirituality which, of course, is so fundamental to this community. Our spirituality, based on messages channelled through Eileen Caddy, references only those chakras from the heart upwards. The lower chakras are simply not recognised. So qualities of love, compassion and consciousness are lauded in the community whilst matters of power, passion and sexuality are not well recognised.

But I believe that change is in the air. The HLSF group is evidence of this. There is a coterie of mostly, but not exclusively, younger members of the community who are more openly discussing and exploring issues of love, intimacy and sexuality. 'Cuddle puddles' are now a feature of many a party, gathering or casual encounter. The tide is shifting in favour of greater openness and transparency. I hope that both this book and the one I published in 2014 can effectively feed into the zeitgeist.

ONE MONTH LATER...

I have now completed the week long, intensive, Tantra training for beginners that I mentioned above. And here is the result... I am totally in love with everyone, everything, indeed the whole damned universe! I feel the sacredness of life and the oneness of it all. I genuinely feel that 'all that I am, is one with all that is' – a phrase repeatedly invoked during the course. And in saying that, I have already disregarded a request made by Jan Day, the Tantra teacher who held the course, that we don't disclose anything about the week to others. So from here on, I'm not going to reveal any more of the content or the detail. I am at liberty, however, to mention how the experience was for me so long as it doesn't directly refer to people and events.

Jan's request is made for good reason. She rightly points out that it's impossible to communicate the full meaning of particular processes or occurrences without setting the context. Each element of the course only makes sense in relation to all the others. Indeed they form an integral package of processes that take participants on a week-long journey of initiation that can only be understood in the doing, the experiencing and the journeying. Reading or hearing about it doesn't, in the slightest way, convey the experience. And apart from that, knowing about the content in advance would spoil the experience for anyone who subsequently decided to do the workshop. At no time during the week were we given a schedule or otherwise told of what was coming next. And that in itself was powerful. Each new step in the journey was a complete surprise. The unfolding of the experience felt like being led on a magical mystery tour.

Five Findhorn Foundation coworkers attended the course. That was another special dimension of the experience for me i.e. undertaking a journey of profound personal discovery with people who were already friends. We deepened our connection immeasurably. And in the case of one particular co-worker, he and I established a heart connection where before there was distance and resistance between us.

I don't know what more I can say really, given the non-disclosure agreement. The venue for the workshop was the gracious Newbold House, a fine late Victorian manor house set in beautiful gardens five miles from Findhorn. Newbold is home to a small intentional community of about a dozen people who live by the same spiritual principles and practices as we do here in Findhorn. Indeed, they are an offspring community. Like us, they run workshops and other programmes throughout the year and provide an excellent B&B service. I'd personally like to thank the Newbold community for their loving care and attention throughout the week. The logistics of hosting such a large workshop can not have been simple. But they ensured that our needs were well met whilst remaining completely inconspicuous, which to my mind is key to successful event hosting.

The night following the end of the course I went with a friend to see the Scottish Ballet perform Tennessee Williams' Streetcar Named Desire, a classic story of love, desire and sexuality. In my heightened state of sensitivity to exactly those aspects of our common humanity, I was totally transfixed and moved by the performance. Gore Vidal said of the original play that it 'changed the concept of sex in America.' How synchronistic that I should attend such a performance the day after completing a Tantra initiation. For I believe Jan's course has likewise changed my conception of my own sexuality. I learned an enormous amount throughout the week, about my long-held sexual attitudes, preoccupations and patterns. Some of the lessons were hard, but all the more beneficial for that. And some of the experience was truly transformative and inspiring. I cannot recommend Jan's courses highly enough. She is a 'master teacher,' as one of the participants said in the closing circle. Her website is www.janday.com.

13

A DIFFERENT KIND OF SHARING

I have previously mentioned a certain kind of 'sharing' that we do here in Findhorn. In groups, typically sitting in a circle around a candle, we 'share' what's going on for us i.e. we talk about our innermost thoughts and feelings and/or what's going on in our lives. This kind of sharing is one of the essential practices we utilise to deepen connection and build relationships. In this chapter, I want to discuss a different, more utilitarian, form of sharing – the trading, lending, borrowing, or gifting of goods and services.

Sharing on the physical plane (i.e. owning or using material items jointly with others) involves explicit or implicit arrangements and agreements made by a group or a subgroup (e.g: an ecovillage or one of its neighbourhoods; a suburb or one of its streets) that enable efficiencies to be developed and/or mutual benefits to be derived. Our carpool, for example, comprises a subgroup of about 70 community members (and a few from out with the ecovillage) who share 10 or 11 late model vehicles including three that are fully electric. I believe that we're the largest private or community owned carpool in Scotland and, as such, we've received significant financial support from the government. I've been a loyal member since it was founded eight years ago. The benefits I derive are too many to elaborate here. Suffice to say that the carpool makes car ownership a joy, rather than an expensive, conflict-ridden burden. And it's a source of pride in what we can achieve collectively.

Sharing builds social relationships but is dependent upon them, in that the degree to which people are willing to share depends upon the trust and goodwill they have established. Willingness to share and cooperate is pervasive in a viable community. It represents the commitment of the group to the ideal of cooperation and is critical to their social development and group cohesion. At Findhorn we already do a lot of this kind of sharing. We collectively own land and numerous community buildings and facilities. Many community members, myself included, live in much smaller dwellings than otherwise we could as a direct consequence of being able to share communal facilities (laundry, guest rooms, office and workshop space etc.). Communal facilities take quite some time, effort and coordination to operate and maintain. Within the Findhorn Foundation the 100+ coworkers share these tasks, either as part of their daily work or as a periodic rota commitment in their own time.

The informal sharing of personal possessions is also strong feature of community life at Findhorn. This kind of sharing reduces each household's need to own and to purchase consumerist items. That I can borrow a juicer for a fast, or a tent to go camping, means I don't need to buy these items and own them outright. However, in this regard I think we could do more, *much* more. I would love to see a more *formalised* system that enables us to share personal possessions and household goods in a more comprehensive and committed manner. Inspired by the example of our carpool, I don't see why we cannot develop a system which makes the sharing of private possessions extensive, efficient, effortless and joyful.

Ten years ago, I published a book on cohousing in the US, Japan and Australasia. At the time I was particularly inspired by one or two communities that had instigated such a system. At Commons on the Alameda in Santa Fe, for example, members had compiled and circulated a list of building, gardening, camping, cooking and other equipment that each household owns and was willing to share. Members would refer to the list should they want to borrow an item and approach one of the relevant households. Below is a excerpt from the list, probably about a third of its entirety. As far as I can tell, there's absolutely no reason why we could not instigate such a system here at Findhorn. Indeed, I think it's extremely remiss that we haven't done so before now.

Category	Item	Lender Unit #	Category	Item	Lender Unit #
Gardening	Hand trowel	A5,A6,B1,B4	Outings	Backpack	A6,A7,B1,C7,D3
	Lawn mower	A6		Bicycle tools	A7,B1,C7,D3
	Leaf rake	A2,A5,A6,B1,B3		Car bike rack	A5,A6,B1,C5,C7
	Weed scythe	C4		Maps	A6,B1,B4,C7,D4
	Wheelbarrow	A2,A4,A6,B1,C4		Snowshoes	D3
Building &	Back belt	A6,B1,B3		Tents	A7,B1,B4,D2,D3
Maintenance	Bucket	CH,B1,B3	Cooking	Coffee pot	A6,D5
	Jigsaw	A6		Oversize mixer	CH,D4
	Sewing machine	A6,B3,B4,C7,D3		Wok	A6,B1,B4,D4
	Staple gun	A6,B1,C7	Other	Blow up bed	C4,D5
	Toilet plunger	A5,B1		Single futon	D5
	Toilet snake	B1		Folding tables	B1,D3,C6,C7
Cleaning	Mini vacuum	A7,C4			
	Rug cleaner	B1	To add your valuables to the list, call Ken.		

I recently listened to an excellent Bioneers pod cast delivered by a Dr Gabor Maté in which he said,

Materialism is a system of belief and behaviour that considers material things, particularly the control and possession of material things, more important than human values such as connection and love, or spiritual values such as recognising the unity of everything.

Maté's words rang a bell. If we turn the quote around, we get something like this:

In Findhorn we believe that human values such as connection and love, and spiritual values such as the unity of everything, are more important than material things, particularly the control and possession of material things.

Well my community, if this really is the case (and surely it is!)

then how about it? Let's demonstrate our professed values by implementing such a system. We already have our 'Boutique,' a place where community members and guests can leave clothing and other personal possessions for others to take, *gratis*. We also have a library of privately donated DVDs and CDs from which anyone can freely borrow. The envisaged system would compliment these valuable, long-standing facilities. It would enable members to retain their possessions whilst also share them with others. Such a system would add significantly to our resilience. It would further the localisation of our economy and reduce our dependence on the global marketplace i.e. enable us to purchase fewer consumerist items produced in those horrendous factories in China and elsewhere.

But what might such a system look like? Might it be paper-based, like the one above, or Internet based? If it's the latter, how do we design a system that doesn't disadvantage or exclude the non-computer literate? If we did go with a digital management system, might we simply adopt an existing platform or find one that allows customisation (such as the one we use for the carpool) or have a system designed and built locally, tailored to our needs (such as our communal meals booking system)? For me there is a danger in innovating for innovations sake. Technology can help, hinder or be irrelevant. I'm interested only in what technology, if any, can best facilitate the activity itself – the sharing!

I've done some research and found that numerous Internet start-up hopefuls have already been working on the idea. There are many digital solutions (Websites) out there that we could utilise. Streetbank, for example, a London-based site with global reach, enables neighbours to exchange all kinds of goods and services. It has only three members within a mile of The Park, but seems to be growing internationally. 'We are starting a movement,' the site claims, 'one built on generosity, friendliness and holding what we own lightly.'

Unfortunately, many of these kinds of Internet-based

initiatives actually monetise the exchange process i.e. they emphasise renting, leasing or hiring rather than lending, borrowing, swapping or gifting. This is perhaps not surprising given that they are mostly developed by digital entrepreneurs looking to capitalise. My feeling is that we are better off with a local initiative designed by community members for our own purposes.

And there is another problem with these sites; they generally don't hold or display an inventory of items that each member owns and is willing to share. If this were the case then a member seeking to borrow say, a tent, would go to the database and search on 'tent'. The names of several tent owners and their addresses would pop up. S/he would then approach one of them and ask to borrow the item. The problem with this arrangement is the vulnerability members might feel in revealing the extent of their worldly possessions (to potential ne're-do-wells). So, in fact, most sites of this type don't work like that; instead they require those seeking an item to put out a request, to which other members who possess such an item are expected to respond. But this, it seems to me, is never going to work as well as a system which requires the seeker of the item to do the leg work. The person with the need is always going to be more motivated to ask to borrow an item than the owner of such an item will be to make an offer. The seeker is motivated by need. The owner's motivation can only be altruism. However, a computer-based system with log-in and password available only to subscribers could work in the former manner. In principle, it would be a digital version of the above paper-based listing which, I believe, would intrinsically be much more likely to succeed.

There are other design questions to be thought through. Would we want to focus on just the borrowing and lending of material goods (like the above system) or might we also include services such as massage, babysitting and computer training? And if the latter, might that undermine some of our own community members who are trying to scratch a living with such skills? And what of the issue of relativity that has long beset time-bank arrangements? Is an hour of babysitting, for example, equivalent to an hour of legal or financial advice? There are other potential concerns. The relatively well-off are able to lend and borrow as a lifestyle choice whilst stigma might attach to those less well resourced with little to offer and greater material need. All of these considerations, and more, are important but they can, I believe, be resolved through thoughtful system design.

There is a burgeoning phenomenon out there called 'collaborative consumption' or the 'sharing economy' that began with the GFC (Global Financial Crisis) of 2008 and is now being fuelled by the ongoing global recession. Some of us might know it as the 'gift economy.' In neighbourhoods and regions all over the world, people (who start out as strangers) are coming together to share. Invariably, they soon realise that there is much more to be gained than just the economic savings; there are also social and environmental advantages. To quote but a few of them: 'The value of sharing is people connecting. It's a social value.' 'It brings people together. It makes people happier.' 'A sustainable society is also one in which we choose positive behaviours that make us feel happier, more connected and more disposed to help others.' [1]

At Findhorn we are already connected; we have already built deep and pervasive trust. We have an awareness of all of the issues. It should be easy for us to instigate such a system. Come on Findhorn! Let's do it!

---

[1] This chapter draws on an excellent report, *Design for Sharing*, by Ann Light and Clodagh Miskely, published November 2014. It's available online.

14

GOVERNANCE, MEETINGS AND
DEEP LISTENING

I've just come from a Findhorn Foundation coworkers' meeting – an assembly of Foundation staff (paid employees), apprentices (those doing our *Living Education Apprenticeship Programme*, LEAP) and invited others. It's the largest regular meeting of FF personnel. Coworker meetings are held on an ad hoc basis every three or four months. They can be called in extraordinary circumstances, or as a means of updating the coworker 'body' with important information, or simply for group building or social purposes. On this occasion, 60 or 70 of us gathered to discuss various matters at hand. We met in the Beechtree Room in Cluny, our second campus in the township of Forres, five miles from Findhorn. I chose to write on this topic (or perhaps the topic chose me) because I came away from the meeting totally inspired by what I witnessed and experienced there. It raised for me, some of the features and qualities of our community that keep my enthusiasm and commitment here alive.

I came to Findhorn 10 years ago following a lifetime spent, on and off, in a diverse range of intentional communities. In each of them I experienced a different mode of governance and approach to meetings. As I've mentioned already, my first communal experience was on kibbutz in Israel in the 1970s. The kibbutz movement was then about 70 years old, very firmly established with time tested systems and procedures. Members would meet once a month at an *asefa* (general meeting) in the dining hall – seated, I recall, at laminated tables set in a very large rectangle under harsh fluorescent lighting. Decisions would be discussed and a vote taken with a show of hands. Whilst this looked ostensibly like direct democracy at work, it also felt formal and alienating. However, there was one feature of kibbutz governance that particularly impressed me. Positions of power were strictly rotated every two years, even the key position of *Merakez Meshek*, a cross between farm manager, finance director and CEO – 'top dog' in other words. The choice of next *Merakez* would be taken more than 12 months in advance. The candidate would be plucked from their job driving a tractor or milking cows and sent away to study for a year before taking up the position. Two years later s/he would find themselves back on the tractor or under the cows. For me, this epitomised the egalitarian ethos that so drew me to kibbutz in the first place. I'm not sure whether it survived the economic crisis that befell kibbutz in the '80s; I'd be surprised. In fact, many aspects of kibbutz life have been completely transformed over the last 30 years. The socialist/egalitarian ideological base has been completely eroded in most cases.

Having left Israel for reasons that I mentioned in a previous chapter, I returned to Australia seeking a new communal lifestyle. By the mid to late 1970s the hippie ethos and alternative, back-to-the-land, movement were kicking off in Australia. Recently married, I moved with my wife to Tuntable Falls, the largest hippie commune in Australia. Tuntable was an anarchic place; it couldn't have been more different to kibbutz in terms of its systems and procedures. In short, there were none! Or at least, very few. As I recall, we had only two rules: that there should be no cats or dogs (in order to protect the wildlife); and also no firearms (in order to preserve the peace and love, brother!). And yet people transgressed both. A few pet owners refused to relinquish their beloved animals and a few others insisted on keeping a .22 so that they could despatch the cats and dogs. But I digress.

We made an attempt at governance. Like kibbutz, we held a general assembly every month for the purpose of decision-making. But that's where the similarities ended. Called a 'Tribal Meeting,' anywhere between 10 and 100, half or fully naked folk would sit on the grass in a circle under a tree. Decision-making was haphazard. There was little protocol to it and even less agreement on any one topic. But it didn't seem to matter much; most of us were too laid back and/or too stoned to care. After eight years my family and I moved away from Tuntable, back into the mainstream. Our reasons were many and varied but one was my disillusion with an alternative lifestyle in terms of its potential for 'world work.' In the beginning, we hippies were terribly idealistic (and also terribly naive, it must be said), convinced that we were going to change the world by our example of a collaborative and sustainable, low-impact lifestyle. In the end, the onset of rampant consumerism and individualism in the '80s rendered our example less and less relevant to the mainstream.

In the early '90s I got excited about what I sensed was the start of a new communal movement that, this time, was fully embedded within the mainstream! Cohousing, as it was called, seemed from what I was reading to have the potential to enable large numbers of regular, urban, middle-class folk to live more simply and collaboratively – downsizing their houses, being less consumerist and more environmentally and socially proactive. I spent eight years as an academic researching cohousing in Denmark, Holland, Canada, Australia, New Zealand, Japan and the US; in the process, visiting 30 or 40 cohousing projects and ecovillages. And in most of them I had the opportunity to sit in their meetings. At the time, consensus decision-making was all the rage and it was applied in *every* group. Consensus was thought to address the deficiencies of conventional processes based on voting, which can discount the views of minorities, leading to alienation, withdrawal from the process and/or non-compliance with any given decision.

The marketing literature of one cohousing community suggested that consensus 'puts all members on an equal footing, avoids power struggles and encourages everyone to participate by communicating openly.' In fact, genuinely open communication (let alone the level of transparency critical to any such process) generally requires a separate and resolute agreement of its own. Many groups had such an agreement, usually written into a mission statement or some other social contract. And this is a point I most wish to stress. In my experience, it's not actually the social technology per se that makes or breaks a decision-making process (i.e. whether it's based on voting, consensus or Sociocracy, for example). In my opinion, successful governance is less dependent on a chosen methodology and much more reliant on deeper, underlying levels of trust and openness in the group. On the whole, I was very impressed with the smooth running of the consensus-based meetings I witnessed, despite the fact that many cohousing groups were in the midst of the often stressful period of designing and constructing their buildings and landscape. Their governance and indeed their social interaction generally was underpinned by high levels of trust and goodwill. This is a feature of cohousing. Members typically come together two or three years before designing, building and moving into their community. They purposefully build relationships of trust and understanding before having to face the challenges of community life.

One of the things that most struck me when I first arrived at Findhorn was the level of grace which pervaded most meetings. Prior to that, I had endured eight years as an academic sitting in faculty meetings driven by inflated egos, hidden agendas and intellectual one-upmanship. At Findhorn, people seemed modest, unassuming and without any hidden agenda. Furthermore, they actually listened to each other!

Meetings of all kinds appeared to run without structure, sometimes without even a chairperson. Usually a 'focaliser' would lead to begin with, but after that, most meetings self organised without need for overt control or intervention. Typically, they became a free-wheeling discussion somehow guided by an invisible protocol: everyone waited their turn to speak; nobody would interject or speak over another; and nobody spoke for longer than appropriate. I was very, very impressed. And it strengthened my conviction that a group with relationships of trust and goodwill doesn't need to overlay their meetings with structure (i.e. use consensus, Sociocracy or something similar). Indeed, it's better off without!

Anyway, back to the coworkers meeting I mentioned. On this occasion it was lightly held by Camilla, our Chair of Management; she had information she wished to convey. There were essentially two topics to cover. Camilla spoke to one and another coworker, Adele who works closely with Camilla, spoke to the other. The first was a very sensitive matter that carried the potential to tip the group into angst and recrimination. The second was a vast and somewhat amorphous topic that probably meant something different to every person in the room. As such, it might have been a difficult topic for 60 people to coherently discuss. And it also carried a certain charge with the potential to incite strong feelings. After Camilla and Adele had talked to each topic, a discussion ensued. Many people spoke, some passionately. Yet, throughout the meeting, a sense of calm, order and deep listening prevailed. The discussion of both topics was completed in good time, with everyone who wished to speak feeling heard. It was very inspiring.

I believe there are two main contributors to this level of grace that characterise our meetings: our agreements and our spirituality. The Findhorn Foundation and Community have developed over many years what we call, the Common Ground. This is a list of 14 agreements that represent values to which we all hold. The Foundation Website says of the

Common Ground, that it's 'a living document, a code of conduct, and used as a tool for transformation for ourselves, the community and the world.' Every FF coworker formally agrees to do their best to abide by the principles articulated in the Common Ground. I'm not going to discuss it here in depth; the full document can be downloaded from the Website (www.findhorn.org). But I'd like to identify those particular clauses which I believe clearly contribute to the grace of our meetings:

1. **Respecting Others**: I wholeheartedly respect other people – their differences, views, origins, backgrounds and issues.
2. **Direct Communication**: I use clear and honest communication with open listening, heart-felt responses, loving acceptance and straightforwardness.
3. **Reflection**: I recognise that anything I see outside myself—any criticisms, irritations or appreciations—may also be reflections of what is inside me.
4. **Nonviolence**: I do not inflict my attitudes or desires on others.
5. **Perspective**: I acknowledge that there may be wider perspectives than my own and deeper issues than those I am immediately aware of.

The second reason for the success of our meetings is, I believe, our spirituality. Our spirituality involves deep 'inner work' i.e. working on, and taking responsibility for one's issues, particularly those things that trigger us. This is where we look deeply into our psyche to identify the source of our aversions, irritations and challenges. We reflect upon our various needs, wants and desires and seek to unpack their origins. And it's where we get to work on the ego, to ensure that its shadow side doesn't suddenly flare up in the middle of a meeting.

Finally, I must admit that we do have an adopted meetings methodology of sorts – we begin all gatherings with a moment of silence. This simple but deeply meaningful act defines our meetings, in a way. It goes beyond helping participants settle into the space and become present. I believe it works very subtly to remind us of our commitment to the Common Ground and also the reflections and results of our 'inner work.' A moment's silence serves to prime a meeting with those qualities I've mentioned: grace, ease, openness and deep listening. At the end of a meeting, we usually link hands and close with another moment of silence, this time to express gratitude for what has transpired. And in that moment, speaking for myself, I also feel the oneness of the group and, for that matter, our community – our essential interconnectedness.

All of these qualities that so impress me about our meetings are what enable them to flow with such grace. So I for one, am strongly opposed to the introduction of Sociocracy as an overlay to our meetings, as is proposed. I don't think we need it, and furthermore, I think it could do more damage than good. It has the potential to stifle the free flowing conversational style that is enabled by our underlying trust and goodwill. Perhaps, there is an argument for using Sociocracy (or whatever is the next big thing in meetings facilitation) on rare occasions, for particular purposes – when a controversial decision needs to be made, for example. But apart from that, I move that we don't adopt it!

15

WILLINGNESS, SERVICE AND WORLDVIEW

For some days I've felt closely accompanied by the Angel of Willingness. This is classic Findhorn-speak. What do we mean by it? Or rather, what do *I* mean by it, for such a feeling must surely be subjective? My interpretation is simple. I'm not naturally drawn to esoteric or mystical meaning or language, unlike many Findhornian friends and colleagues. As mentioned before, I've held a strongly material and sceptical worldview my whole life. So in saying, 'I've been accompanied in the last few days by the Angel of Willingness,' I simply mean that I've several times witnessed an act of extraordinary willingness by people around me. Or perhaps, the quality of willingness has shown itself more often, more clearly, or more strongly than usual. And in a community where acting willingly in service is one of the highest values, this means a lot. Given the community context, to have been particularly inspired by singular acts of service, or several of them, is significant – significant enough to inspire this chapter.

If I were seeking a more Findhornian interpretation of the presence of the Angel of Willingness, I would immediately refer to the booklet that accompanies a pack of Angel Cards. Angel Cards I described in some detail in Chapter 4. They were originally created as part of the Transformation Game, invented here in Findhorn by Kathy Tyler and Joy Drake in the '70s, but have since become popular in various guises all around the world. Angel Cards (the original ones) each carry a word representing a particular quality or value, and a sketch of an angel somehow enacting that quality. In the case of Willingness, the card's message according to the accompanying booklet is the following:

> Approach life with an open mind and a how-can-we-make-it-work attitude. Use your will skilfully to enhance the creative process rather than inhibit it.

So the spiritual message carried by the Angel of Willingness is: keep an open mind, adopt a can-do attitude and be creative. Ironically perhaps, the picture on the card shows an angel washing the dishes…

As mentioned, acting with willingness is normative behaviour around here and a strong part of the culture. And service, per se, is written into our code of conduct, the Common Ground, specifically in Clause 2: 'Service: I bring an attitude of service to others and to our planet, recognising I must also consider my own needs.' It is commonplace for people here to go out of their way to freely serve or support (without expectation of recompense of reciprocation) the people around them or their organisation, the community, humanity or the Earth. It's a spiritual practice of sorts, one that we hold in common with many of the world's faiths. So what was it that particularly inspired me to write a chapter on willingness? What were those extraordinary demonstrations of open mindedness, can-do-ism and creativity?

My week began with one of our regular, un-extraordinary acts of service – well two actually. On Saturday I had Saturday Homecare. This is a rota commitment that comes around once every three weeks. All residential Findhorn Foundation coworkers participate. We spend an hour or two on a Saturday morning cleaning our guest accommodation during the very short, two hour window between one week's guests departing and the next arriving. Then on Sunday, I participated in another rota – washing dishes after Sunday brunch. This comes around once every couple of months. This week we had a large turnout at brunch so KP (Kitchen Party, as we call it) took a good two hours. Neither of these acts of service was remarkable, although having them both fall on the same weekend is unusual. But perhaps worth mentioning is that both were truly enjoyable. Cleaning toilets and washing dishes are not my favourite activities, to be sure, but doing the work collaboratively in a team and knowing that it contributes to the viability of the Foundation makes all the difference. In that context, acts of service become a joy and a privilege.

No, the act of willingness that particularly inspired me came at work, in my job in the Conference Office of the Findhorn Foundation. My current preoccupation there is with a big event coming up in July, the GEN+20 Summit. We are expecting between 300 and 400 participants; it could be our biggest conference for 20 years. In the week prior, we are planning several short workshops which we thought would appeal to some conference goers and encourage them to come for an extra few days. We had originally scheduled six of these workshops, but we discovered on Monday morning that another which should have been included was not, through no fault of our own. In the meantime the two presenters of this seventh workshop have been promoting it around the world for the last twelve months!

What to do? The process of including a workshop in our

annual programme is very complex; it involves at least three departments, many personnel, and a lot of staff time and trouble. The programme information has to be entered into a central database and included in our brochure and on our Website. It also needs budgeting and setting up on a Bookings database. There is considerable administration required in the months leading up to the workshop running, not to mention the ongoing work required by our Homecare, Kitchens and Gardens Departments in accommodating and feeding the participants. I was doubtful that I'd be able to gain the consent of everyone involved to include the workshop as a favour to the presenters. And I was expecting the process of negotiation to take days. But by lunch time, I had the enthusiastic agreement of all concerned, even though they are all very busy and the late inclusion will involve considerable extra work on their part. I was quite astonished that everyone involved expressed such total willingness, and so spontaneously. Their how-can-we-make-it-work attitude was well in evidence.

In my role as a project manager of the GEN+20 Summit, I'm currently seeking volunteers for some of the crucial roles. We need to find two experienced Head Ushers (to manage the ushering in the main conference venue, the Universal Hall), two Teas Focalisers (to organise the tea breaks), people to administer two conference registration sessions, others to manage the many venues etc. etc. There are about 20 of these key positions, all of them requiring quite some commitment of time and effort. During a big conference the felt responsibility and inherent stress levels in these positions can be very high. And yet we offer no payment for this kind of work; it's purely voluntary. Those who volunteer, do it out of the goodness of their heart and because they know that our conferences are important 'world work.' Their contribution is an act of service, not only to the FF or the community but to the world. On the white board in the Conference Office we currently have written 'healing the world, one conference at a time.' This is how we feel about our work. We see that it brings profound and lasting change and transformation to the people attending and also those participating via Web streaming. Anyway, on Monday, I sent out about a dozen emails to people we know that have experience in those key roles. I asked whether they'd be interested in taking on the position yet again; most of them having done the job time after time. And yet, within a couple of days I had harvested nothing but positive responses from almost all of them. Again, I was impressed and inspired by their willingness and their selfless attitude of service to the Foundation, our community and beyond.

These separate instances of willingness and freely offered service may not count for much in and of themselves, but when they come as thick and fast as they have this week, I'm given cause to reflect and appreciate. What may seem like isolated instances are not really separate and distinct. They are connected via the 'field' (zeitgeist) – the commonality of thought and action that pervades the community of Findhorn. Being immersed in a field of common purpose is itself, an inspiration. It provides extra motivation to offer even more service to the cause.

If this chapter is beginning to sound zealous or preachy for someone with a supposedly sceptical world view, let me explain why I am affected so. As mentioned already, at a very young age, around 12 I think, I rejected the notion of a Judeo-Christian God and replaced a religious code of conduct with a homespun frame of my own. The core of my ethos was, and still is: to fulfil my potential in creativity, service and love. (For more about this refer to Chapter 1). So the practice of service has always been central to my worldview. This is, in part, why I feel so at home in Findhorn. And for that matter, my mission to fulfil my potential in love and creativity is also very well supported by the culture here.

Which reminds me – it's time for dinner in the Community Centre, to be followed by my weekly Thursday night KP rota – yet another opportunity to actually *become* that Angel of Willingness washing the dishes.

PART THREE

WORLD WORK

16

ESALEN MASSAGE

In this final section, I turn to matters beyond the personal and interpersonal; I look more closely at the 'world work' we do at Findhorn based mostly on our programme of courses, conferences and other events. I begin with an account of how it was for me to be a participant in one of our own courses – a week long introduction to the style of massage developed at the famous Esalen Institute in California. I hope that my writing about the experience will offer a glimpse of how it is to be involved in one of our programmes as a guest. I can't say, 'a typical programme,' because this one was very different to most, and in any case, each course is unique, although some of the activities I'll describe below are common to many.

I have always been a keen amateur masseur. I love the sense of touch and the communication that skin to skin contact brings with another. And yet I've never undertaken any training to learn how to do it with more understanding and purpose. My approach has always been very intuitive. And whilst this has served well enough, I have always wanted to strengthen the effectiveness of my technique. Without knowing much about it, Esalen Massage has appealed especially in recent years as I've spoken with trainees undertaking courses here in Findhorn. However, I've never been able to afford the cost of the full month-long training. This week-long introduction, at a subsidised price for Findhorn Foundation coworkers, is very affordable and in perfect timing given that my workload in the office is light at the moment.

I arrived at Cluny, our campus in Forres where the Esalen courses are run, mid-morning on Saturday. Registration was quick and easy. I meet the lovely Mika, our trainer who has come all the way from Tokyo for the purpose and her co-facilitator, Nadashree whom I already know well as a Foundation coworker and a good friend. I was allocated a very nice room, facing south, overlooking the beautiful Cluny gardens and the golf course beyond. Before lunch I unpacked and made myself at home there, then mingled with a few of the other participants. We scratched the surface of each other's worlds, learning names and countries and backgrounds, gaining a sense of with whom we would journey for the next week. Lunch was typically beautifully conceived and prepared, Findhorn style. I sat to eat at the long table in the bay window at the far end of the dining room, the same table I had adopted during Experience Week – the viewpoint from which I originally fell in love with the gardens and landscape around here.

We met as a group for the first time at 2pm in Cluny's Ballroom, our home for the week. This is a magnificent Victorian room with a high, richly decorated ceiling, teak panelling on the walls, magnificent large windows, fine wooden floor and a spaciousness bordering on grandeur that belies its compact size. It's my second favourite interior space in this whole region; the first being the aforementioned dining room. The purpose of the first session, as it is with almost all our programmes, is an introduction to the course and to each other. It quickly becomes clear that we are a very diverse group in terms of massage experience. Several are already practitioners and teachers of massage therapy and an equal number have little or no experience. One participant has never given or received a massage in her life and was even a little anxious about being touched. I wonder how much of a challenge such diversity will pose for the focalisers.

After an hour or so of preliminaries we move to the Sanctuary for an Angel Meditation. This is something we integrate into almost all our courses. It's an attunement of sorts whereby a focaliser will lead a meditation, inviting the participants to go inside to align, then select (or perhaps it selects them) a card from a deck which portrays a particular quality that will accompany them during the week. I drew the Angel Card of Grace – always a lovely quality to dance with. What's not to like about Grace?! And the Angel Card selected for the group as a whole, the Group Angel, was Light. We shared what our respective qualities meant to us – whether they resonated or not, or touched on something going on in our lives. Then we completed the session by forming a circle and going inside to individually and collectively express gratitude for the events of the day, for life, for anything really that we fancy appreciating. This manner of closing a session is common to most group activities held in the community.

Saturday evening is one of the two nights of the week when the sauna in Cluny is fired up. So after dinner, that's what I did. And it was delicious. More than adequately hot, with a very cold outdoor plunge pool and a lovely wood-lined rest area, the Cluny sauna is a much valued facility, certainly by those hardcore sauna-goers who regularly meet there.

Sunday morning was to be the first day of the course proper; but rather than launch straight into a session of massage, we began with an hour of meditation and yoga. This is unusual for our courses. Participants on most of our programmes always have the option of attending our regular morning group meditations in the two sanctuaries at Cluny and The Park. But it's rare for there to be a morning mediation followed by yoga held by the course focalisers. Both activities were beautifully led by Mika. Then we broke for a light breakfast and returned to the Ballroom for the second session of the day; once again, this was not a massage session. Rather, it was an hour-long session of dance, again lead by Mika. And so it's been every morning this week; we would start the day with meditation (half an hour), yoga (half an hour) and dance (an hour). The emphasis on self-knowing and healing through meditation, yoga and movement is part of the Esalen ethos. They rightly believe it's essential that massage practitioners develop a deep awareness of their own physicality and also consciously attend to their emotional and spiritual well-being.

At 2pm, we met again for the first session of massage. During the check-in, more than a little frustration was expressed that it had taken 24 hours to get to this point. I was feeling a little of that, but because of my understanding and appreciation of the 'field-setting' that is part of almost all our programmes, I was predominantly feeling relaxed and grateful to be there. Mika began by explaining then demonstrating a few basic strokes on her 'client,' Nadashree – actually, just one long continuous stroke down the back from shoulders to buttocks, up the sides and across the upper back to the shoulders, then back to the neck and head. It became clear to me in an instant, that YES! this is a style of massage that I can enthusiastically adopt; strokes that are deep, long, continuous, fluid and very, very slow, bordering on sensual, that are surely deeply relaxing and healing for the lucky recipient. Mika demonstrated a stroke or two more. She used her whole body at fullest stretch, sometimes with feet firmly planted, using gravity's pull on her bodyweight to provide the impetus and strength to her strokes. And at other times, up on her toes and pirouetting like a dancer around shoulder or foot as she completed the pulled stroke along arm or leg. It seemed that this massage style would be as much of a joy to give, as to receive.

We paired up to practice on each other. My partner was a good friend from within the community so there was little apprehension as we set about applying what we had witnessed. We worked on each other for about a half hour, applying the strokes we had observed whilst being closely supervised by Mika and Nadashree. I was in heaven, learning how to do with intent and purpose what I'd always done with intuition and love. I now feel (several days later) that I'll be able to blend all of these incentives to confidently offer a massage to friends and lovers that will bring them relaxation and healing. The ensuing days of the course followed the same pattern. We began with meditation, yoga and dance, followed by two sessions of instruction and the giving and receiving of massage. I have no intention to take further Esalen massage courses. I doubt that I will ever be able to afford the full month's training but, in any case, I have no desire to turn this new interest into a vocation. This week has been perfect. It has provided sufficient input and inspiration for me to now be able to offer a full-body massage with reasonable understanding and proficiency.

17

BUILDING BRIDGES

The previous chapter was about a course held here at Findhorn written from my perspective as a participant. In this one, I want to tell a similar story, of the unfolding of another Findhorn event, but from the viewpoint of the (co)focaliser – someone who organises, holds and steers. The programme is one that we crafted especially for a visiting group. It's specific to the needs of the group, not something we offer for general consumption in our brochure or on our website. We have always held such tailored events; there have always been single interest groups coming to us for fact-finding or inspiration-harvesting visits. But historically we handled such requests on an *ad hoc* basis; somehow, somebody would magically cobble together and run a programme for them. A few years ago, however, in the face of increasing numbers of such visits, we created a brand new department called Building Bridges (BB), dedicated to overseeing such programmes.

The three coworkers who staff BB are tasked with a) creating and coordinating bespoke programmes for groups that invite themselves to Findhorn, and b) proposing and seeking funding for programmes designed especially for groups of people with special needs. The creation of BB has brought much greater rigour and professionalism to the way we deal with groups who self-invite. And also, it's delivered new kinds of programmes for people who, because of the cards that life had dealt them, wouldn't otherwise have the resources or the opportunity to visit our community. This second type of visit is typically funded by local government as part of their social services programme. Participants might, for example, be marginalised youth of the region or folk with learning disabilities. Building Bridges has ensured that our visitor demographic has become much more diverse in recent years. This is great in terms of developing our 'reach' and it also brings extra richness to our lives as the residents here. I, for one, am very grateful for their work.

Anyway, a couple of weeks ago, I received an invitation from BB to join one of their team, Edward, in focalising a programme for a Norwegian delegation coming for just four days in late October. I was told they were a group of about 20 involved in, or somehow associated with, the development of an ecovillage located in the countryside north of Oslo. The instigators of the visit, I was told, are two of the founders of the project and they're bringing several architects, some local politicians including the mayor of their municipality and a film crew working on a four part documentary for Norwegian television called *Ecovillage*. The proposal sounded just like my 'cup of tea' I have an architectural background (as a practitioner and educator) so I am always keen to engage with visiting architects to both show them what we have achieved here but also to learn about their projects and their work, particularly in the fields of sustainable and community architecture. I knew that my regular workload in the Findhorn Foundation Conference Office would be relatively light at that time so I replied to the invitation with a resounding YES!

Much of the planning for the visit had already been done by the time I came onboard, otherwise, to be honest, the programme created might have been somewhat different. The schedule I was sent seemed reasonable, however I suggested a few tweaks which were graciously implemented by the BB team. I should mention too, that much of the agenda setting had been driven by the two founders of Hurdal Ecovillage, one of whom had visited Findhorn some 30 years earlier as a 16 year old and been so inspired he had received a vision of a future, Findhorn like, Norwegian community. It took another 20 or so years for the project to crystallise, but now it's well on its way to realisation. Currently, there are 100 people living on site and the project is on track to fulfil the founders' vision of a full-featured ecovillage of about five hundred souls, dynamically integrated into the surrounding region.

And this is where the local politicians come in. The delegation includes three: the local mayor, his deputy and the municipality's Head of Administration (who, in her words, is tasked with implementing the directives of the other two). The municipality of Hurdal lies in the Romerike region of Norway; its administrative centre is the small town of Hurdal, on the outskirts of which, the ecovillage of Hurdal is located. The Mayor, Runar Bålsrud, has a strong vision of his own, I learned yesterday on the first day of their visit. He is passionate about sustainable development and is striving to create the first truly 'green' municipality in the country. As yet, I don't know much of the detail of Runar's ambition. So I've just taken a look at the municipality's Web site and even though there is no English translation, I could glean from the array of clickable icons that the vision is already on track. The very first of the pictograms is a rubbish bin, the second is a recycling truck, and the third is a greenhouse. This is exactly the kind of politician we just *love* to receive here at Findhorn.

It is very confirming of our 'world work' to be reminded that Findhorn has influence well beyond the self-referencing world of intentional communities – that we can and do inspire positive change in wider, mainstream, society. Because ultimately, of course, that is where change simply must happen. Only a tiny (but happily, not irrelevant) proportion of the world's population will be privileged enough to live in sustainable (intentional) communities like ours. In my opinion, it is crucial that leaders and change makers make every effort to bring sustainable community to the mainstream and to the cities if there is to be any kind of agreeable future for our world. And this, of course, is the core purpose of the Building Bridges department. To this end, it is extremely gratifying to have this delegation accompanied by a film crew of the Norwegian national broadcaster (their equivalent of the BBC). The documentary they are making will spread our influence and inspiration up and down the land of Norway and perhaps beyond.

Prior to their arrival on Saturday afternoon, I was feeling apprehensive. Presenting to architects is always a little two-edged for me. I know how they think, and that causes me to sometimes feel quite apologetic for the architecture here at Findhorn. For historical reasons, we have never had much of a master plan for the development of housing and infrastructure. We inherited a caravan park of unhealthy, unsustainable buildings. Many of them, well past their used by date, still exist. And the building programme has unfolded in a very ad hoc fashion, resulting in a mix of styles that reflect the different interests and preoccupations of the people involved at the time. Whilst the architectural informality might appeal to many visitors, I expect that most architects find our built environment lacking in cohesion. (Keven McLeod once said of our settlement that it looked like it had been designed by Willy Wonka Architects.) Added to that, the presence of high level politicians in the group and the filming of the visit for television put me a little on edge.

They arrived at about 2pm by coach from Aberdeen airport. We met and welcomed them on the 'runway' – that remnant 20 meter wide strip of concrete and tarmac that has, by default, become our main car park. It's called that because during the Second World War it was built to enable fighter planes to be taxied around and dispersed in the landscape to prevent them easily being destroyed by enemy bombers. This is another aspect of our 'planning' that irks me and for which I feel apologetic. The first impression gained by most visitors to our community is their arrival into a bloody great carpark – not a good look for any self-respecting ecovillage.

We provided a light lunch in the Community Centre, registered them all (but for two who had been delayed in coming and would arrive late) and showed them to their accommodation. They dropped their bags and we escorted them to our meeting room for the duration of the visit, the Park Lecture Room. The PLR is one of my favourite venues; it features wonderful picture windows facing into the woods. I have done a lot of teaching in the space and feel very much at home there.

We began with an attunement led by Edward. This is always a bit of an edge with groups as mainstream as this one. Sitting in a circle around a candle with eyes closed whilst someone invokes the presence of angelic beings is a new and sometimes challenging experience for many people. And we had gained an impression from Kristin that she'd prefer us to downplay the more spiritual aspects of our culture, I assumed because of the presence of the politicians and camera crew. But the group seemed to take it in their stride. We followed up with a round of introductions. Everyone in turn stated their name and reason for being on the trip, whether it be as ecovillage residents, architects, builders or regional politician. The group appeared to comprise genuine, engaged and open individuals. I began to relax. I took an immediate shine to the Mayor; he seemed modest and unassuming for a politician.

For the next hour I presented a slide show and talk about our community in all its various facets. Time didn't allow for much dialogue; I would have preferred a more discursive exchange, yet the presentation was well received. We set out on a brief tour of the community, elaborating on aspects of our history and culture in such historically significant places as the Original Garden, Universal Hall and Nature Sanctuary. Following dinner, the day ended with a talk and discussion led by Alex Walker, a long-standing member of the community who has been centrally involved in much of its physical and economic development. Alex sparked a lively discussion and fielded many questions. I felt satisfied by the end of the day that, one way or another, the group had received a thorough introduction to our community.

Day two comprised a series of presentations and discussions with key members of the community. The instigators of the visit had made it clear at the outset that they were most interested in how our community integrated with the surrounding region and related with various levels of government. So we organised four speakers: Kosha Joubert, President of the Global Ecovillage Network; May East, CEO of CIFAL Scotland and Findhorn's delegate to the UN; Carin Schwartz, founder of Transition Town Forres, and; Camilla Bredal-Pedersen, Chair of Management of the Findhorn Foundation. That the speakers were all female did not escape attention. It's clear that a disproportionate number of the most influential members of our community are women. These four passionate and committed women filled our guests with so much information and inspiration that they were left reeling by the end of the day. In addition to the talks, we fitted in a tour to Transition Town Forres and to Cluny Hill, our campus in Forres. It was a full and fruitful day. The evening was free but by coincidence, the Nordic Fiddlers Bloc, a band playing traditional Scandinavian music, were appearing in the Hall. I think most of the group went to the gig. I didn't; I was too knackered, but I heard the next day that a good time was had by all.

The final full day of the visit began with a tour of our sustainable housing, including visits inside of four very different buildings: my ecomobile; Edward's house (9/10 Bagend) shared by 8 coworkers; Auriel's barrel house; and Michael and Gail's splendid new home in Soillse. The group were engaged and curious. The diversity of our housing is in

105

distinct contrast to theirs. Their houses are all built to the same design, albeit with variations of size. By standardising they gained efficiency of production, relative affordability, reduced stress for the home buyers and architectural cohesion for the project.

Following the tour we had the opportunity to hear from them about their project in Hurdal. Simen, the founder, gave a comprehensive presentation that was followed by a short presentation by Runar, the Mayor, about his government's ambition to effect carbon neutrality in their municipality by 2025. In the afternoon, the group enjoyed something different – the chance to literally get their hands dirty in Cullerne Gardens, weeding and preparing a field for planting a new winter crop. These kinds of 'group projects,' we call them, offer guests the opportunity to experience the life and culture of a work department and apply our principle ethos, 'work is love in action.'

In the evening, we held a 'completion sharing' in the Earth Lodge, a circular six meter wide space half buried in the ground with a central fire pit and hole in the roof for the smoke to escape; it's a kiva (native American ceremonial and social space) of sorts. The gathering was intended as an opportunity to enjoy some singing and music making, and also share some final reflections and appreciations. Craig Gibsone, community elder, permaculturist and expert didge player led some chanting and Kristin sang a beautiful traditional Norwegian song. The sharing was very deep, profound in some cases. A strong camaraderie was felt and expressed by many – a linking of minds and hearts across the North Sea. We were all moved, some of us to tears. It was a beautiful, soulful way to complete.

All in all, it was a short, packed and intense programme that certainly satisfied our 'clients' and helped forge new links of friendship and support between our ecovillages. I very much enjoyed the opportunity; working with Edward was a delight. I hope it's not the last time I'm recruited at short notice by Building Bridges.

18

THE NEW STORY SUMMIT

The New Story Summit (NSS) was a week long conference held here at Findhorn between Sept 27th and Oct 4th, 2014. Its none too small agenda, was to seek to unfold a 'new story' for humankind. As a Findhorn Foundation coworker employed in the Conference Office, I was centrally involved in the organisation of this event for most of the year. One of the joys of my job is having the opportunity to see come to fruition, months and months of dreaming, planning and sustained hard work. And with this event, the satisfaction in seeing a successful outcome was immense, such was the logistical complexity involved. The organisers had taken a major leap of faith in leaving much the programme unplanned and pregnant with possibility. How could an event seeking to develop a New Story be otherwise? What emerged was deep, powerful and chaotic.

The context for this event was, on one level, the rolling programme of conferences and events held by the Findhorn Foundation. The FF is a charitable trust with education for a better world (in a broad sense) at the centre of its charter. These major events occur every two or three months. We also hold a myriad of courses and workshops; two or three every week of the year. Most of these are week-long whilst a few are one month or even three months in duration. This is the core business of the Foundation, upon which it's reliant for its financial viability. And it's events like the NSS that make by far the largest contribution to our budgetary bottom line. So it's all the more significant that this event was held under Gift Economy conditions, meaning that participants did not register to attend in the usual way, paying a fixed fee of between £600 and £1000 (depending on income). Rather they were required to pay a nominal registration fee of £50 (minimum) and then, at the end of the event, attune to what more, if anything, they wished to contribute. In the very last session, we offered participants this opportunity and we waited in curiosity and a little apprehension, to see whether or not the NSS produced a much needed surplus. We needn't have worried. The event was a financial success, delivering a healthy surplus. Interestingly though, about 70% of the participants gifted less than the cost would normally be to attend such an event. We made a surplus because 20% of the participants gifted generously, two of them, extraordinarily so.

That aside, the conference was a great success on many, many levels. The participants numbered around 320, making it the largest event we've held for twenty years. Usually our conferences attract between 100 and 200 participants. So the logistics were commensurately complex; all of our support systems were strained to the limit. Our kitchens normally cook for a maximum of one or two hundred guests at a time. Our in-house accommodation is limited to about 120 beds. Our main conference venue, the Universal Hall, is limited in its capacity and we have only a handful of smaller spaces for break-out sessions and workshops. Our Homecare, Gardens and Maintenance departments have a well established remit and routine that does not normally vary greatly. However, for this event, we had to throw out the norms and protocols and embrace all manner of augmentation, innovation and improvisation. And we the collective, including the wider community beyond the Foundation, did so hugely successfully, I'm pleased and proud to say.

Mind you, we were greatly assisted by the superb weather. In late September-early October it's entirely possible that the weather be cold, wet and windy. Temperatures can be as low as zero deg C. And this is what we had planned for. However, for the whole week, up until the Friday night, we had brilliant sunny skies and temperatures in the high teens. This enabled many people to eat meals outdoors on the terrace and lawn, even at dinner time. So the pressure on the Community Centre dining room was greatly relieved and the large marquee that we had hired for the overflow was hardly used. The benign conditions also ensured that workshops, rituals and all kinds of gatherings were able to be held outdoors. And of course, the warm weather lifted everyone's spirits, not least those participants who had come from Africa and equatorial Asian and South American countries.

On that matter, the diversity of participants at this event was like none other in the history of our community. The organisers had invested considerable effort in fundraising over US$100K to bring our brothers and sisters from the Global South to the event, including many indigenous folk. Initially, up to 80 were invited from Africa, Asia, the Americas and Australia. Sadly many of them were refused an entry visa by the ultra-cautious (to put it kindly) UK Border Control; ultimately I think only about 50 arrived. But their presence was profound. The indigenous elders led several powerful rituals, which I for one did not imagine would suit an event focused on a New Story for humankind. But I was absolutely wrong. The wise ones were there to remind us of those human qualities that will be absolutely essential as we move forward into an era of extreme climate change: humility, cooperation, loyalty, compassion and love.

The live Web-streaming was another very successful aspect of this event, with thousands of people, many of them organised into 'hubs,' watching the event unfold from afar. And many of those hubs then conducted their own programme of talks and workshops to tease out for themselves what a New Story might look like in their part of the world. Because ultimately, our survival of the coming climate crisis will best be met with a multiplicity of localised responses tailored by the activists and inhabitants of each bioregion. This for me was one of the principle 'findings' of the New Story Summit. And in that sense, it's an *old* New Story. I remember as a hippie in the '70s advocating, and indeed living, exactly the same vision. Let's hope that this time around we can make some progress down that route. We have no choice now.

.

19

HEALTHY BIRTH – HEALTHY EARTH

I was in Australia recently on holiday with family when something came up that inspired this chapter. The topic? No less than the role of community in the evolution of our species. Yes, I do see a link there! So this chapter is not about Findhorn directly, but about community life in general and its contribution to the making of a better world through the humane welcoming of babies and raising of children. So if some of what follows feels like the self-indulgent ramblings of a proud dad and doting grandpa (which it is) then please bear with me. I will get to the point eventually.

I spent time there with my daughter Anna, her partner Tom and their then, five month year old baby, Mattea, my second grandchild. My other daughter, Liberty and her partner, Bradley have a one and half year old son called Gus. Anna and Tom live in a beautiful timber and mud-brick house set in sub-tropical rainforest in Northern NSW not far from where Anna and Liberty grew up. In fact the house is very much like the one they were born and raised in (until they were eight and six years old, respectively), a house that I built over several years on the hippie commune, Tuntable Falls. Tuntable is still (I think) Australia's largest intentional community – some 150 people living simply and sustainably on about 1200 acres of beautiful land near a town called

Nimbin, NSW. My ex-wife, Jane, and I lived there between 1977 and 1984.

Anna was born at home a few months after we moved to Tuntable. I had to work feverishly prior to her birth to construct the first stage of the house. We moved in a few days before the birth and she was born, serenely and naturally with midwife and birthing team in attendance and a dozen or so friends and neighbours looking on. A couple of years later, Liberty was born in similar circumstances – at home, quietly, peacefully and naturally.

By that time, Jane had become a doula and lay midwife as a member of the same birthing team that attended our two home births. I would often accompany her when she was out attending a birth as both our babies were breast fed well into their second year. I would look after them whilst she worked, presenting them for feeding as necessary. I was (and still am) a keen photographer and was often asked to shoot these births. It was such a privilege, being the team photographer; births generally, but particularly home births, are extremely photogenic, such is the atmosphere of ecstatic joy and serenity that usually pervades.

These were idyllic years for us. We were living the dream. Anna and Lib grew up in what I think of as perfect circumstances: close to nature; with both parents at home most of the time; in a handmade house with few consumerist mod-cons; within a hamlet of other families with similarly aged kids; in an intentional community with a social and environmental purpose. We grew much of our own food and sourced fresh, local, organic produce otherwise. We spent time sitting in the sun socialising, playing or listening to music, swimming in the river and hanging out. With their playmates and from a very young age, the girls freely roamed the property unsupervised by adults. They had dozens of surrogate mums, dads and grandparents all around to shower them with love and attention. Their peer group was a young tribe, growing up in the loving embrace of the community at large, which was a tribe in itself.

Life for the kids was way beyond good. And as a direct result, I believe, Anna and Liberty grew up to be emotionally intelligent, open-hearted and compassionate adults with progressive, humanitarian values and ideals. In their work as adults, they have sought to make the world a better, more humane place – to bring love and light to those in need. Their interests and proclivities took Anna into anthropology (working with aboriginal communities in Central Australia) and Lib into midwifery (working mostly with underprivileged immigrant women in New Zealand). Anna and Lib have always gathered loyal and devoted friends and colleagues about them; through their being so loving, they inspire love in others.

It's through this life experience (watching my kids grow up) that I've come to firmly believe that birthing and raising children in community is the single greatest contribution we can make to creating a more peaceful and loving world. And also, it is the communities movement's single greatest contribution to the creation of a more sustainable future for the planet. In short, the *conscious* conception, gestation, birthing and raising of children is crucial to: the making of loving and caring human beings; the creation, therefore, of a civilised and sustainable society; and so, the saving and healing of the planet.

This conviction has led me to join with two colleagues in organising a conference on the topic in September 2016. Called, 'Healthy Birth – Healthy Earth,' the event will draw, we hope, over 300 birthing professionals, academics, parents, prospective parents and interested others to Findhorn for a week of talks, workshops, classes and cultural events (films, performances, celebrations etc.). The conference theme is this nexus between *birth* and the *Earth*. The three of us, the core conference team, met recently to develop our ideas. These are the basic principles we agreed upon – our 'manifesto':

- How we are born affects both our capacity to love and be aware.
- Babies learn during gestation and birth whether the world

is safe or terrifying.

- Birthing mothers are the environment supporting and nourishing future generations who will determine the health of the planet.
- Crises in birthing practices and the environment stem from the objectification of matter – either as a woman to be controlled or a planet to be exploited.
- Healing relationships with our mother, birthing mothers and Mother Earth lie at the core of a sustainable future.

What, specifically, has inspired this chapter? Well, my granddaughter Mattie and I have been hanging out. She is only five months old, but it's already very clear to me that she has acquired many of the same character traits that I ascribed to my daughters above. She is open, affable, contented, loving, present with others and as serene as could be. In the few days I was staying with them, I hardly heard a peep of complaint from her, let alone a cry. So it got me thinking that there might there be a 'second-generation effect' going on here. Mattie has many of the same influences upon her that Anna and Liberty had as children. Anna and Tom are super-parents: they are both at home (Anna is a full-time mum at the moment and Tom works from home); they shower Mattie with love and attention; and they lead a gentle, quiet, spiritual kind of life in their beautiful handmade house, close to nature and in community.

The family live on land shared with a few other households, yet there is little interaction amongst them. However the property is close to a progressive small town called Mullumbimby, in an area that's renowned for its sense of community. All about, there are numerous intentional communities and all manner of collectives and individuals leading 'alternative lifestyles.' It's 21st Century hippiedom! The whole of far North Eastern NSW, which includes the towns of Nimbin, Mullumbimby and Byron Bay, is known as the Rainbow Region for this reason. I could digress here into a rave about how the hippie movement was sparked in

Australia by the famous 1973 Aquarius Festival in Nimbin. But I won't.

Anyway, Anna and Tom have many thoughtful, gentle friends in the area. They enjoy a nurturing local culture, one in which loving acceptance and open-heartedness are the means of exchange. One evening whilst I was staying with them, we attended the launch of a new café in Byron Bay. The event was held in an industrial building converted into a venue for community-based cultural development called Kulchajam. It was lively and well attended by a hundred or so 'alternatives' – chilled-out folk dressed casually, interacting open-heartedly, being their authentic unconventional selves.

There was no cover charge. The evening was alcohol free. The somewhat chaotic kitchen was serving delicious, wholesome, vegetarian food, for free! Entertainers were performing for free! Artists were displaying their work on the walls as a gesture of support. It occurred to me that the whole event was being run on a gift-economy basis (which as an aside, Tom in his volunteer role as treasurer of the organising non-profit, was not fully convinced was a viable approach).

Inspired by all this, Anna and I were volunteering in the kitchen. When I wasn't washing dishes, I was socialising and enjoying the art and music. Some of the time I carried Mattie around. The atmosphere was way more lively than she is used to at home. The music was loud at times, kids were running around excitedly, adults were engaging with gusto. And yet she was quietly wide-eyed and curious, not phased by the chaos, smiling at strangers and being her usual happy self. To me, this demonstrated an impressive level of resilience. Despite having lived a very quiet, peaceful life since she was born, she had no trouble coping with an entirely different and potentially disturbing atmosphere.

So, it set me wondering! Anna told me of something she'd read which claimed that certain human genetic defects can be bred out of existence within a few generations. Perhaps then, it might only take a few generations of our kids repeatedly enjoying a humane and loving welcome into community for peace, harmony and resilience to become the norm. And in the process, perhaps we will gain a critical mass of people who will love and care sufficiently for each other and the planet to make a difference. Yes, 'I'm a dreamer, but I'm not the only one.' There are millions of us living in communities all around the world who are working, whether we know it or not, on this very same project.

May love prevail.

Photograph by Anna Meltzer

20

MOUNTAIN WALK

These final two chapters are both completely off topic in the sense that they are not about Findhorn at all or even about community living. They are about my experience of Scotland – the rural and the urban. I have included them in a book about our community because I believe in the importance of context. The Findhorn community is international and in that sense, could be situated anywhere. The demographic profile of residents and guests gives no indication of it being located in Scotland. And yet to me, its location is highly relevant. I can not imagine living in any intentional community that I felt was disconnected from it's surrounding culture and landscape.

I am a New Zealander by birth; I grew up there. But I spent almost my entire adult life in Australia. On hearing this, people often ask me why I choose to live in Scotland when I could be living in Australia – the implication being that Australia has a lot more to offer. The question usually comes from someone who doesn't know me well (or at all); often, for example, in a lunchtime conversation with an Experience Week guest. I can only imagine that they are thinking something like: Australia = warm weather, Scotland = cold weather; Australia = New World, Scotland = Old Country; Australia = land of opportunity, Scotland = dead end, etc.

The question is both easy to answer and tough to rationalise. The easy answer is I'm here because I have chosen to live in the Findhorn community and ecovillage, of which there is no equivalent in Australia. I hope that this book has made it clear why this is so important to me. The difficulty I have with it (and my greatest challenge) is something they haven't usually considered. I have family in Australia: an aging mum whose health is not the best; two married daughters whom I love with my whole being (one in Oz and the other in NZ); two grandchildren whom I am watching grow up via Skype; and several siblings, as well. To be living in Scotland, about as far from them as it's possible to get, is hugely difficult and conflicting.

But the Findhorn community is just my primary reason for living here. I doubt whether I could if I really hated the weather and found Scotland alienating. But actually, the opposite is true. I love this land: its nature, history, culture and politics. I can handle the weather here and I love the seasonality that it brings. What's more, I don't at all appreciate much of the history, culture and especially the politics of Australia. I find all of that totally alienating. And I struggle with the weather there more than I do in Scotland. One can at least dress appropriately for a Scottish winter. I find it more difficult to endure a typical Australian summer. So for the moment at least, I am very happy to live in Scotland, despite the challenges. I am committed to be here until at least the end of 2016. If the pull back to Australia is much greater by then, and Tony Abbot is no longer Prime Minister, I will consider returning there to be closer to family. In the meantime, I deal with the separation by travelling there once a year and stay in touch courtesy of the Internet. But of course it's hard.

All of this is by way of introduction to this chapter. I wanted to report on a mountain walk I did with friends two days ago. But before doing so, I'd just like to expand a little more on my love of all things Scottish. I have been here 10 years now and am fully enamoured. Actually, it's living in Europe that I enjoy as much but that's another story. I have permanent residency in the UK and hope to gain citizenship within a year. I recently registered to vote for the first time in my life (having always been a conscientious objector to party politics) just so that I could vote for Scottish independence. I am fascinated by Scotland's history and culture. I love golf. And I adore the landscapes. What more can I say? Scotland rocks!

It's the extraordinary landscapes, in particular, that I associate with my adopted home country, and that they are so pristine and undeveloped. Scotland is very under-populated. In North Scotland anyway, there is little noticeable ongoing change to either rural or urban environments. The countryside appears to be almost completely free from development; even new houses here look like old ones! There is hardly any traffic on the roads. And the Highland landscapes in particular are exquisitely beautiful to my mind. Some people find them alienating due to the scarcity of trees. But I find them extraordinary! Let me see if I can illustrate.

Two days ago, I set out with four friends to spend a day hiking in the mountains. We drove about an hour from Findhorn to a town called Aviemore, a famous Highland destination for hikers, skiers and nature lovers. We drove on another 15 minutes, almost to the base of Mount Cairngorm, Scotland's most well known winter skiing destination. In summer the area is popular for its flora, fauna, water sports and walking and hiking opportunities. We planned to climb, not Cairngorm itself (4080 ft), but the much less challenging *Meall A'Bhuachaille* (2650 ft) which, honestly, is just a foothill. But it's perfect for a relatively easy mountain walking experience in beautiful, diverse landscapes and ecosystems. The whole area, although mostly privately owned (some would say stolen by the landed gentry i.e. the English aristocracy) is a National Park – indeed Britain's largest. Cairngorms National Park covering 4,528 square km was established in 2003 under the National Parks (Scotland) Act 2000.

We set out from Glenmore Visitor Centre, headed uphill through plantation pine forest and also areas that had been clear-felled where the vegetation was struggling to re-establish. Sadness was expressed by those who could see little regrowth since the last visit two years earlier. Once we got above the tree line the landscape changed radically and the views opened up. At this time of year, the heather is in full bloom. So for the next hour we walked through a lush lavender coloured carpet of heather up a recently constructed path-cum-stairway of local stone. Further up the mountain we met National Parks volunteers who were valiantly extending the route.

As we came closer to the top, the heather gave way to a barren, rocky (shale) moonscape. And the wind started to howl. It amazed me how we had no consciousness of the wind until we neared the summit and then, suddenly, without any apparent change in the weather, it became a gale. Easy to see how ill prepared or inexperienced, but occasionally even expert, hikers can get caught and sometimes perish in these mountains. I was glad I'd borrowed good quality outdoor gear from a work colleague. It was very cold, although not quite the minus seven degrees (with wind chill factor) that I'd seen forecast.

At the top, we sheltered in a ruined bothy (a wee stone hut) with several other hikers, all wearing brightly coloured mountain clothing. We, and they, pulled out our packed lunches of sandwiches, fruit, nuts, chocolate and thermoses of tea. We were high on the experience and ate mostly in reverent silence. It was a bit like a ritual of the inducted ones. And I felt honoured to be amongst them.

The 360 degree views were stunning; visibility was good. We could see countless other mountains, hills and valleys and about a dozen blue and green lochs scattered all about – with hardly a road or a building as far as the eye could see. We could see wet weather all around us and had the privilege of watched it moving rapidly across the landscape. If you're in it, of course, you don't get that opportunity. And we could see some heading our way. So after eating, we posed for the obligatory group selfie and headed back down, but by a different route.

We descended the other side of the mountain with the wind at our backs. I was grateful for the walking poles I'd borrowed. It felt like they stood between me and being blown all the way down. But once down a hundred feet or so, the wind died as quickly as it had sprung up on the ascent. We could see a tiny wee lake, Lochan Uaine, way down the bottom which was our next destination. Along the way we stopped briefly at an intact bothy – one of those facilities provided free by National Parks for hikers and skiers to take shelter in or perhaps sleep overnight. The interior was minimalist in the extreme, with just a fireplace and a built-in wooden window seat. I could live in it, I thought!

We stopped next at Lochan Uaine, a mysterious phenomenon actually. It's one of those rare lochs without a water course running into or out of it. There was an eerie green colour to the water and what seemed like submerged ramparts, which turned out to be huge bleached logs, not far from shore. We investigated an area of woods with a dense undergrowth of ferns and brackens. The path led to a recently constructed platform and seat overlooking the loch, the perfect place for an impromptu céilidh (traditional Scottish dance). A member of the group, a guy I had not previously met, showed himself to be an excellent whistle player. The rest of us danced as light rain began to fall. It was a sweet moment.

We pressed on; the weather was threatening. We chose a return route through what's called, the Caledonian Reserve. Remnant old growth Caledonian forest contains ancient native Scots pines (up to 500 years old) and a range of other trees, including junipers, birches, willows, rowan and aspens. They are powerful awe-inspiring places, dense with vegetation and wildlife. We walked in single-file and silence but for the accompaniment of Ian's tin whistle, up and down along a narrow stone pathway that passed close by some incredibly gnarled old trees. The thick vegetation was wet and pungent.

The whole thing felt to me like a clip from Lord of the Rings. Indeed, I think it took me back to childhood and hiking in dense New Zealand rainforest. I *loved* it!

We got back to the car all too soon, drove back to Aviemore for a snack and then headed for home. The atmosphere in the car was one of deep nourishment and contentment – tired bodies and engaged minds, high on nature and the company. We vowed to do it again soon. I can't wait!.

21

SCOTLAND, YES!

I'd like to expand upon comments I made in the last chapter about my love of my adopted country and, for that matter, Europe in general. Even though I grew up in NZ and later lived in Australia, I have always felt much more strongly drawn to living in Europe. And I know exactly what the attraction is; it's the visibility and accessibility of the history and heritage that I feel here. NZ and Australia both have ancient indigenous cultures of course, but neither Maori nor Aboriginal history is very accessible to an uninitiated white fella. And visual evidence for it is not much found in cities. In Europe, on the other hand, history is written into the very fabric of cities. One just needs to walk down any High Street, linger in any back alley, or loiter anywhere near the centre of most cities to sense the heritage of the place and its people.

In my experience, that same *genius loci* is nowhere to be found in Australia and NZ. The urban fabric does not evidence the change and adaptation that represents the passing of time and building of collective memory. The cities are simply not old enough.

I was prompted to write on this topic because I recently spent a weekend in St Andrews, a traditional Scottish seaside town famous for two things – its university and the game of golf. For a life-long golfer and once academic, the place has tremendous appeal; I love St Andrews. It's a compact city, very walkable and almost unchanged in terms of its layout and scale for a thousand years. Most buildings in the centre of town are at least 500 years old. Some go back much further.

The now ruined St Andrews' cathedral, for example, was once the most important religious site in the whole of Europe, attracting pilgrims from all over the continent. Consecrated by Robert the Bruce around 1300, the cathedral and consequently the town flourished for the next 250 years. But at the height of the Reformation in the 1500s, the building was trashed by a Protestant mob following a rousing sermon by firebrand preacher, John Knox. The building was abandoned and the stonework became a source of recycled construction material for the region.

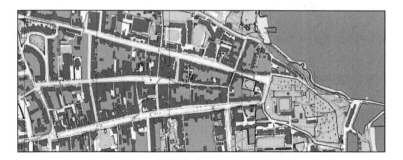

Still standing tall amongst the ruins is the 1000 year old tower of St Rule's Church, a building that preceded the cathedral. The top affords stunning 360 degree views of the cathedral site, town, ocean and harbour. The town's three main streets, North, South and Market Streets, are set on axis with the cathedral and tower which in medieval times would have guided pilgrims to their destination. North and South Streets are both lined with ancient university buildings looking like mini-Hogwarts with their towers and battlements. Between them lies Market Street, lined with small specialty shops, narrow at the ends but broadened in the middle to form a marketplace. The whole ensemble of streets and buildings 'speaks' (nay, 'shouts') to me of a thriving medieval life of religious fervour, academic learning and bustling street action. Furthermore, the layered and patched stonework – the visible evidence of recycling and reuse over many centuries – tells stories of successive periods of human progress followed inevitably by periods of decline. This is what I love, most of all, about living in Europe – being at once reminded of the luminosity and achievement, as well as the frailty and impermanence, of what it is to be human.

Scotland's two best known cities are, of course, Edinburgh and Glasgow. And what different places they are. I love them both, but for quite different reasons. Edinburgh is, at its core, another medieval city. Glasgow is a much more modern and mercantile place. Edinburgh has, in fact, a split personality – the old and the new. The Old Town, centred around the Royal Mile and Castle, is famous for its urban density, steep narrow lanes and street life. The Royal Mile forms a spine anchored at each end by two buildings that couldn't be more different. Edinburgh Castle is located at its head and the new architecturally 'out there' parliamentary building at its base. Between them lies a mile of historical and cultural magic, particularly during August when the world's most famous festival of the arts completely takes over the town. I have been to three Edinburgh Festivals, two in the '70s and one much more recently. I count them amongst the most memorable experiences of my life.

Edinburgh's New Town is separated from the Old by a narrow but topographically dramatic strip of open green space. New Town is as distinctive as the Old but strongly contrasting, with its formal street layout, splendid Georgian architecture and unified urban fabric. Set amongst it are some wonderful opportunities for adventure and escape. One of my favourites is Leith Walk, which passes almost secretly through a densely vegetated ravine with a deep and fast-flowing river. It leads to the Scottish National Gallery of Modern Art which is really two galleries in one, both distinctive in their own right for their neo-classical architecture housing some quite radical contemporary art. They are separated from each other by a road and an engaging work of land art created by Charles Jenks.

Edinburgh is, in fact, a city bursting with art galleries. One of my favourites is the National Portrait Gallery, another distinctive historical building, recently refurbished in slick, minimalist style. The contrast between new and old could not be more stark, but the intervention is all the more successful for that. And then there are Edinburgh's two most visited art museums (mostly, I think, because of their location in middle of that nature strip between the Old and New Towns): the Royal Scottish Academy and the Scottish National Gallery. And these are just the large institutional galleries. There are a myriad of small private galleries as well. Edinburgh really is a city for the art lover.

But the *House* for an Art Lover is in Glasgow, a city which for me means just one thing – architect, Charles Rennie Mackintosh. CRM is one of my architectural heroes; I adore his work. He was designing around the beginning of the Twentieth Century. This was the period of Art Nouveau and Mackintosh was the foremost proponent of the style in Britain. He was very much aided by his wife Margaret McDonald, a talent behind much of his decorative work. But Mackintosh was not just a designer of eye candy. He was one of the first pioneers of modernism – one of the few architects of his generation to embrace and combine the decorative and symbolic elements of Art Nouveau with the restraint and functionality of modernism. In so doing, he melded two ostensibly incongruous styles. The two buildings which I most admire for this wizardry are the House for and Art Lover and the Glasgow School of Arts.

The House for an Art Lover was designed for a competition in 1901 but not built until 1996. The building is not as Mackintosh would have envisaged, given that it was built 100 years later than intended and is a tourist attraction with a shop and cafe. But still, it well demonstrates his amazing capacity to synthesise beauty and functionalism. It's a modernist building in conception but exquisitely beautiful in its detailing and ornamentation – so beautiful, in fact, that I am moved to tears whenever I visit. I wept recently for the School of Arts too, but for an entirely different reason. Last May, it was gutted by fire. Designed between 1896 and 1906, The GSA is considered CRM's finest work, similarly exhibiting his talent for synthesising the decorative with the modern. Its library in particular, was one of the most revered architectural creations of any era, anywhere in the world. The library is now entirely gone, although if things go according to plan it will be faithfully reconstructed when the building is restored.

I want to complete this mini-tour of my favourite Scottish art and architecture with something different; else you might get the impression that all art establishments in Scotland are housed in 100+ year old buildings. The Burrell Collection is different; it's displayed in a superb contemporary building designed in the 1970s. In 2013, the building was A-listed by Historic Scotland in recognition of it being one of the country's best examples of '70s architecture. It's beautifully set within a Glaswegian park and thoroughly integrated into the surrounding landscape. Huge outer walls of continuous glazing fill the building with light and offers sweeping views across parkland and into surrounding woods. The small design team included a Norwegian woman, Brit Andresson, who immigrated to Australia soon after the building was completed. There she taught architecture for 40 years. Brit was one of my professors in the '80s. She was a real inspiration, responsible for cultivating (along with others) a distinctive 'Queensland Style' through her own work and also her pedagogy. I can still remember the lecture she delivered on the Burrell Collection building. I resolved at the time to one day visit the building, which I've now just done some 30 years later.

Last year, Scotland voted in a referendum to determine its independence. At the time, the locals talked of little else. I imagine that the media were similarly obsessed although I really have no idea; these days I get my news only from a few carefully selected Web sites. But that's not to say I was disinterested. Quite the contrary; I felt so strongly about this issue that it caused me to register to vote for the first time in my life. Yes, that's right, I have never ever voted, even though I lived for 30 years in Australia where voting is compulsory. I have been, until recently a conscientious objector to voting. Such is my level of disdain for mainstream politics. My attitude was formed well before I became eligible to vote at age 21. When I was 18, the Australian government sought to conscript me to fight in Vietnam, a war which I anyway abhorred. Fortunately, my birthday was not drawn from the hat in their ridiculous ballot. Not that I would have gone, had it been. As a student radical, I was deeply involved in helping conscripts escape the draft. And around the same time I also was resisting Apartheid with a criminal vigour that could have had me locked up for years. But that's another story – one that won't be told here. Suffice to say that my political views precluded voting back then and, indeed, have done so ever since, until last year when I voted in the independence referendum. I voted YES! Why? For me the matter was simple. As I've already said, in this chapter and a previous one, I've developed a deep love for Scotland – so much so that I can even appreciate its mainstream politics. The Labour Party has taken the majority of seats in Scotland in every election since the '60s (until the last one, when they were routed by the SNP in the recent General Election. But seriously, Scotland is a uniquely magical place with a distinctive history and culture. It's different to the rest of Britain in so many affirming ways. So why shouldn't its people have the right to self-determination? As for the detail of the argument, I can do no better than to quote George Monbiot who writes for the Guardian newspaper....

> To vote no is to choose to live under a political system that sustains one of the rich world's highest levels of inequality and deprivation. This is a system in which all major parties are complicit, which offers no obvious exit from a model that privileges neoliberal economics over other aspirations. It treats the natural world, civic life, equality, public health and effective public services as dispensable luxuries, and the freedom of the rich to exploit the poor as non-negotiable.... Independence, as more Scots are beginning to see, offers people an opportunity to rewrite the political rules. To create a written constitution, the very process of which is engaging and transformative. To build an economy of benefit to everyone. To promote cohesion, social justice, the defence of the living planet and an end to wars of choice.

I rest my case, well George's actually.

CONCLUDING THOUGHTS

I was recently asked to write a short piece for the 25th anniversary issue of Diggers & Dreamers, the UK directory of communal living. The topic: 'What is the purpose of communal living?' In one sense I think the question misses the point. To my mind, communal living doesn't need to be justified, defended or even celebrated in terms of its purpose. I see communal living as a default setting i.e. it's the most natural way for human beings to cohabitate. It should be the norm, and of course it was, up until the Industrial Revolution some 300 years ago. For millennia beforehand, we mostly lived as fully interdependent, mutually supportive members of tribes, hamlets, villages and towns. And we lived sustainably! If present day communal living has a purpose at all, then perhaps it's to remind us of this now forgotten fact.

Particularly over the last 150 years, a sense of oneself as an integrated member of society has been supplanted with a measure of one's economic worth, which has in turn been closely associated with status and power. Human values have fundamentally shifted from the social and cultural to the economic and material. Most recently, human need has been dissociated from social satisfaction and cultural meaning; it's aligned instead with consumption, not only of commodities, but also 'entertainment' and substances. Never mind that this trend has fuelled global warming and climate change; it's more than enough that it has eroded our innate capacity for creativity, service and love.

If we are to regain our basic humanity then the specious satisfaction offered by consumption needs to be replaced by satisfactions that are non-material. Communal settlements are the perfect setting for replacing psychological attachment to material gain with location-based social fulfilment and cultural rejuvenation. Anti-consumerist values are, in fact, common amongst members of intentional communities and axiomatic for many sectarian, egalitarian and alternative lifestyle groups. Intentional communities model a more humane, pro-social, values-based way of life. In so doing, they encourage a return to a more modest, measured and, dare I say, spiritual way of life.

Findhorn, is an enduring, practical example of exactly this kind of values inversion and lifestyle transformation. As such, it inspires change and transformation in thousands of visitors every year and is a 'beacon' for many more around the world. And of course we are not perfect; far from it. But we are constantly working on it, striving for the 'highest and the best.' And we are doing so with love! I hope this book has offered a wee glimpse of life inside our community, both the joys and the challenges. Come visit us and experience it for yourself! And if you have any questions, please don't hesitate to contact me by email at graham.meltzer@findhorn.org.

Love and blessings,
Graham

ABOUT THE AUTHOR

I'm a community junkie! I have an abiding passion for community life that's been alive in me for 50 years, since I was a teenager. Here is a little about my life-long engagement with communal living.

I grew up in Auckland, New Zealand where my family was one of six that shared a green space at some distance from the road. We kids roamed freely there as a 'pack' for hours after school and on weekends. The social cohesion and shared values of our post-war suburban community lent security and assurance to life. Added to this, a large extended family and close-knit Jewish community provided a wellspring of love and support from which I benefit to this day. I think my sense of the value and nourishment inherent in community life was established at this time.

As a student during the late 1960s and early '70s I lived in politically radical urban communes where I first experienced shared ideology and purpose. This was followed by three years on kibbutz in Israel during which I became convinced of the immeasurable value of collaboration as a means of achieving both social and material satisfaction. There seemed to me at the time to be a profound connection between the psycho-social and the material dimensions of community life. It took 30 more years of experience and investigation before I could fully articulate what was then just a hunch.

I returned to Australia in 1976 seeking a communal lifestyle. I soon met and married my equally idealistic partner, Jane, and together we joined Australia's largest and best know intentional community, Tuntable Falls, near Nimbin in Northern NSW. The late '70s in Australia was a halcyon period of greatest 'new-age' idealism. At the time, Nimbin was at the epicentre of the dream. We were, we believed, going to change the world by our example of an environmentally responsible community of communities, as self-sufficient as possible, materially, culturally, socially and economically. And for a time there, we were on track!

Living at Tuntable cemented my belief that a nurturing extended family or 'tribe' is the ideal social grouping for the human species and that a socially cohesive group of individuals (some related by blood but most, probably not) has the potential to be a profound milieu for the socialisation of both children and adults. Furthermore, an appropriately sized group, thus socialised, has the opportunity to create a truly civilised and civil society. I saw communalism as the best chance of fulfilling our individual and collective potential for creativity, intelligence, compassion and love – all those wonderful human attributes that, for the most part, remain sadly unfulfilled.

After eight years at Tuntable I returned to university to study architecture. I anticipated becoming one of those 'barefoot' architects dedicated to environmental and/or community architecture. As it happened, I moved quickly into post-graduate study and a full-time academic position teaching sustainable and community architecture. Academia offered the opportunity to apply rigour to previous musings about a link between the social and the material, or as I then saw it, the communal and the environmental. At that time, in the early '90s, there was considerable literature highlighting the incapacity of well-intentioned 'greens' to 'walk their environmentalist talk'. Yet, there was little investigation of the role of social relationships and social satisfaction in underpinning environmental behaviours and practices. I set about such an investigation.

Eight years of part-time research and analysis resulted in a PhD that indeed substantiated a correlation between the social cohesion of a human group and the capacity of its members to enact their environmentalist aspirations. Four more years of occasional fieldwork and part-time writing resulted in a book titled, Sustainable Community: Learning from the Cohousing Model (Trafford Press, 2005). In total, the fieldwork I conducted comprised eighteen months of living in cohousing in Denmark, North America, New Zealand, Australia and Japan.

I left the university in 2000 to take up commercial (architectural) photography. Whilst this went well for five years, I eventually decided I wasn't cut out for business and that my values (communitarian, humanist, egalitarian) were just too much at odds with those of the mainstream. I felt that I needed to get back into community. So I looked around the world for a community to join and short-listed four that interested me, Twin Oaks (US), Ganas (US), ZEGG (Germany) and Findhorn. I visited each of them for a few weeks and ultimately selected Findhorn. I've been here ever since, almost ten years, and am deeply contented. More so, I think, as each day goes by.

Other books by Graham Meltzer
(all available on Amazon)

Another Kind of Space:
Creating Ecological Dwellings and Environments (2003)
(co-authored with Alan Dearling)

Sustainable Community:
Learning from the Cohousing Model (2005)

Deepening Love, Sex & Intimacy:
A True Story (2014)